Growing tasty tropical plants*

*in any home, anywhere.

Growing tasty tropical plants*

(like lemons, limes, citrons, grapefruit, kumquats, sunquats, tahitian oranges, barbados cherries, figs, guavas, dragon fruit, miracle berries, olives, passion fruit, coffee, chocolate, tea, black pepper, cinnamon, vanilla, and more...)

*in any home, anywhere.

Laurelynn G. Martin and **Byron E. Martin**

Storey Publishing

**The mission of Storey Publishing is to serve our customers by
publishing practical information that encourages
personal independence in harmony with the environment.**

Edited by Gwen Steege and Fern Marshall Bradley
Art direction and book design by Dan O. Williams
Production design by Patrick Barber/McGuire Barber Design

Back cover photography by © Adam Mastoon Photography
Interior photography credits appear below
Illustrations by © Beverly Duncan

Recipes reviewed by Andrea Chesman
Indexed by Christine R. Lindemer, Boston Road Communications

Storey Publishing
210 MASS MoCA Way
North Adams, MA 01247
www.storey.com

Printed in China by R.R. Donnelley
10 9 8 7 6 5 4 3 2 1
Library of Congress Cataloging-in-Publication Data
Martin, Byron, 1953–
 Growing tasty tropical plants in any home, anywhere / Byron E. Martin and Laurelynn G. Martin.
   p. cm.
 Includes index.
 ISBN 978-1-60342-577-3 (pbk. : alk. paper)
 1. Food crops. 2. Tropical plants. 3. Plants, Edible. I. Martin, Laurelynn G., 1961– II. Title.
SB175.M37 2010
635—dc22
                    2010022532

Interior photography courtesy of the authors: 19, 21 right, 23, 25 top right and bottom, 27, 29, 31 top right and bottom, 35 right, 37 right, 39 top right and bottom left, 41, 43, 45, 47, 53, 55, 57, 59, 61 top, 63 left, 65 top right, 67, 68, 69, 71 top and bottom left, 73 right, 75, 79, 81, 83, 85, 87, 88, 89, 91, 93, 95, 97, 99, 101, 103 left, 107, 109, 111, 113, 117, 119, 121, 123

Additional interior photography by © Alan Crostwaite/World of Stock: 39 top left; © Food Collection/StockFood: 103 right; © Goss Images/Alamy: 31 left; © Martin Hughes-Jones/GAP Photos: 65 top left; © David Karp and Toni Siebert, Citrus variety collection, University of California at Riverside: 35 left, 37 left, 39 bottom right, 49; © Alia Luria/iStockphoto.com: 61 bottom; © Patrick Lynch/Alamy: 65 bottom left; © Andy Maluche/OnAsia:60; © Adam Mastoon Photography: 2, 6, 11, 12, 15, 32–33, 124; © Sean McFall: 25 top left; © Myrone/Flickr: 63 right; © deb roby/Flickr: 31 center; © Smend/StockFood Munich: 73 left; © Robert Walls/Alamy: 71 bottom right; Wikimedia Commons: 21 left, 65 bottom right, 77

For all gardeners everywhere:

May the process of gardening be the reward,

and the bearing of fruit, the acknowledgment.

In memory of Big Bob, Robert H. Glass,

a Florida plant-collecting companion,

but more importantly a father.

1934–2009

Contents

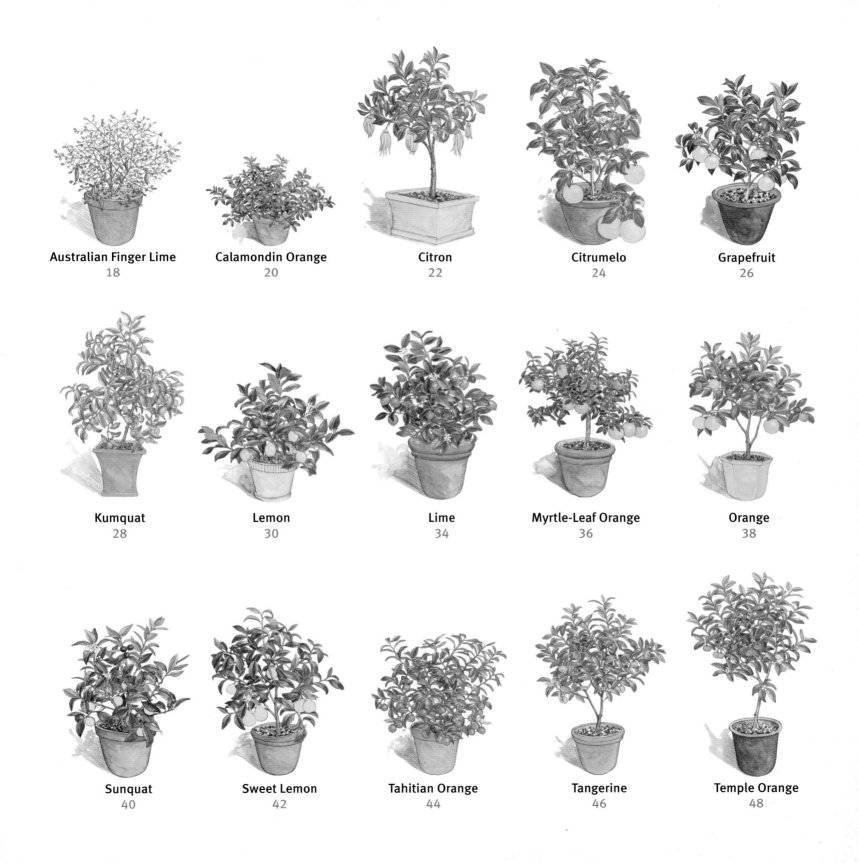

Australian Finger Lime
18

Calamondin Orange
20

Citron
22

Citrumelo
24

Grapefruit
26

Kumquat
28

Lemon
30

Lime
34

Myrtle-Leaf Orange
36

Orange
38

Sunquat
40

Sweet Lemon
42

Tahitian Orange
44

Tangerine
46

Temple Orange
48

Acerola
52

Australian Beach Cherry
54

Avocado
56

Banana
58

Dragon Fruit
62

Dwarf Pomegranate
64

Fig
66

Guava
70

June Plum
72

Miracle Berry
74

Naranjilla
76

Noni
78

Olive
80

Orangeberry
82

Papaya
84

Passion Fruit
86

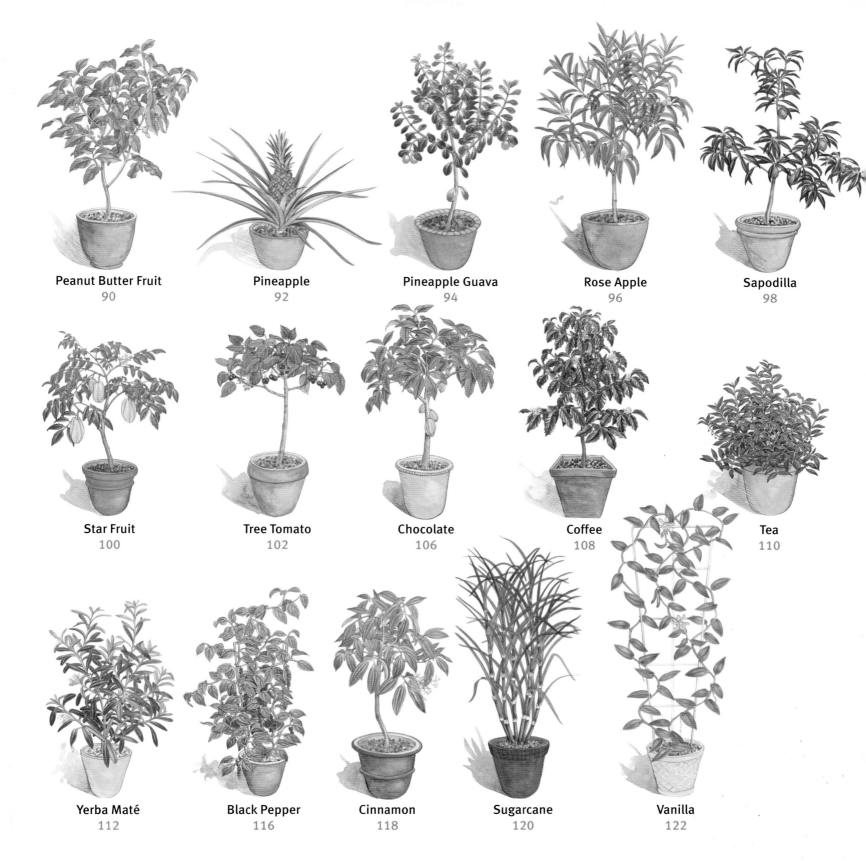

Peanut Butter Fruit
90

Pineapple
92

Pineapple Guava
94

Rose Apple
96

Sapodilla
98

Star Fruit
100

Tree Tomato
102

Chocolate
106

Coffee
108

Tea
110

Yerba Maté
112

Black Pepper
116

Cinnamon
118

Sugarcane
120

Vanilla
122

Enjoying an Indoor Edible Oasis

Orange kumquats drip from a tabletop tree. Ripe bananas wait to be picked for breakfast. Red beans decorate coffee plant stems until plucked for roasting. Growing tropical fruit plants in pots, no matter where you live, adds ornamental beauty and luscious, out-of-the-ordinary foods to your household.

Growing your own food in containers indoors and on your deck or patio not only gives you a healthier lifestyle, but also allows the natural order of plants to become ever present in your daily life. Through this book, we hope to enable you to enjoy a taste of the tropics without leaving the comfort of your home and backyard. We have chosen plants that will grow well in containers in all areas of the country, inside during the winter and outside during the summer. (Southern gardeners can raise some of these plants outdoors year-round.)

Raising fruiting trees, shrubs, and vines in containers is a great gardening adventure. You can grow favorite fruits that you know you like to eat, such as oranges and figs, or experiment with exotic flavors and textures such as dragon fruit and naranjilla. We've also included instructions for growing plants that produce some favorite treats and spices, including coffee, chocolate, cinnamon,

and vanilla. One thing that all of the plants in this book have in common is that they will produce a reasonably abundant crop when grown in containers. With pruning, they can be kept small enough to grow indoors, either on a windowsill or in a sunroom. The plants and varieties featured span the gamut in cultural requirements from easy and quickly rewarding plants such as tree tomato and potted fig trees to long-term endeavors such as a chocolate tree or a potted avocado.

One of the keys to success with tropical container fruits is providing the right environment for the plants as they grow and mature. Some types need a winter cool period, while others do best in warm conditions year-round. Some tropicals can do well in partial sun, but many of them will produce fruit well only when they grow in very bright conditions, such as a sunny windowsill, sunroom, or conservatory during the winter. If you don't have a sunroom or some large south-facing windows, then

you'll need to explore using supplemental lighting for these plants.

For the summer, we highly recommend moving tropicals outdoors to a sunny deck or patio, or even into the garden, where they can serve as a focal point. For example, the large leaves and impressively fast growth of a banana plant make it an ideal focal point in an outdoor garden. Or try naranjilla, with its full dense growth habit and fuzzy orange fruit.

The Logee family has been growing tropicals in containers for generations, and we can't imagine life without them. In this book, we've included all of the best tips and ideas we've discovered for getting the most from these plants, including how to manage watering and fertilizing, when and how to prune, and much more. As you travel these pages with us, we hope we inspire within you the joy and wonderment

RIGHT: Variegated calamondin orange puts on an ornamental show year-round.

of growing tropical plants and that you take a moment to rest into the beauty and abundance of life that these fruiting plants have to offer.

How to Use This Book

Whether you're a seasoned gardener or a first-time grower, you'll appreciate the easy-to-follow instructions throughout this book on how to grow, harvest, and care for your tropical fruit plants in small pots. We've included all the basics you need to know to succeed, and we've taken things a step further by including some of our favorite recipes and other fascinating tidbits, such as how to cure olives and roast your own coffee beans. We've even included the recipe for our special Logee's Meyer Lemonade with a twist of kaffir lime.

Which Plants Do You Want to Grow?

One of the most important choices that this book can help you with is which tropical edible plants you most want to grow. Of course, if you had unlimited space and time, you'd grow them all! But since you don't, study the descriptions of each plant you find appealing. Take note of how large it will grow, how much fruit it will produce, and the growing conditions and any special care, such as hand-pollination, the plant will need. If you're brand-new to container gardening, it's a good idea to start with plants that grow quickly and can tolerate a range of temperatures. If you're a veteran gardener with a sunroom

LEFT: 'TR Hovey' papaya grows rapidly: it can produce large fruit clusters within 10 months.

or small greenhouse, you'll probably enjoy branching out with some of the more unusual plants. Whether you're a beginner or an experienced gardener, refer to the plant lists on page 14 for help in making plant choices.

Tips for Success, Plant by Plant

Once you've decided which plants you want to grow, carefully study the individual entry for each plant. It covers all of the essential care information for the plant, from watering and feeding to pruning and pollination. Each of the plant entries includes an illustration of the plant to help you imagine how it might look inside your home. To tempt you, there are also luscious photographs of the ripe fruit — you'll be amazed at the variety in fruit forms and colors.

The Plant Particulars section of each entry covers plant size, form, origin, and botanical family and what time of year the plant will flower and bear fruit. The Growing Conditions section tells you what light and potting soil the plant needs, as well as the minimum indoor temperature the plant can tolerate. We've also included the outdoor hardiness limit for Southern gardeners who might want to try planting some of these plants in the ground outdoors (many are hardy only in Zone 10, but a few can tolerate winters as cold as Zone 8).

The Care section focuses on fertilizing and pruning, two of the most important aspects of container plant care. And Potential Problems lists the pest, foliar disease, and root disease problems that you may encounter (the good news is

that many of the plants in this book rarely suffer from any serious pest or disease problems when grown in containers).

Giving Your Plants Top-Notch Care

We think you'll find caring for your container fruit plants fun and easy. But new gardeners just starting out and experienced gardeners who want a refresher will appreciate part 5, Plant Care. Here we offer you our time-tested experience on all aspects of plant care. We've included an analysis of the types of containers and instructions for repotting. You'll learn how to tell when your plants need watering and how much water they need. And you'll find detailed advice on fertilizers and feeding, based on whether your plants are heavy feeders, moderate feeders, or light feeders. From there we cover pruning and propagation methods. To round out this section on plant care, you'll find in-depth control information for the eight most common container plant pests as well as descriptions of common disease problems and how to avoid them. We conclude this section with a troubleshooting guide where we provide answers to the questions we're most commonly asked about tropical fruiting plants.

Finding Plants and Supplies

When you've read your fill and you're ready to get started, check the resources (page 155). There you'll find contact information for nurseries in the United States and Canada that sell tropical plants, as well as organizations that are rich sources of information about these amazing and beautiful plants.

Best Bets for Beginners

These plants are a great choice for first-time container gardeners and for any gardener who wants a gardening project that will provide results quickly and reliably. These plants all should produce fruit within a year after you obtain them, and they're not prone to pest or disease problems.

- Coffee (page 108)
- Fig (page 66)
- 'Meyer' lemon (page 30)
- Naranjilla (page 76)
- Orangeberry (page 82)
- Tree tomato (page 102)
- Yerba maté (page 112)

Fantastic Flavors

These plants are sure to satisfy those with a refined palate or simply anyone who loves exquisite flavor. Some are easy to grow, such as coffee plant and sugarcane, while others need a little more care, including sunquat, rose apple, and cinnamon.

- Australian finger lime (page 18)
- Cinnamon (page 118)
- Coffee (page 108)
- Rose apple (page 96)
- Sugarcane (page 120)
- Sunquat (page 40)

Great Plants for Greenhouses

Plants in this category are great for greenhouses because they perform better if allowed to grow large. For example, dragon fruit and vanilla need to form a lengthy vine before fruiting takes place. The other fruits listed here will bloom and set fruit in small pots, but when given the room to expand, they will produce more abundantly.

- Avocado (page 56)
- Banana (page 58)
- Chocolate (page 106)
- Dragon fruit (page 62)
- June plum (page 72)
- Papaya (page 84)
- Star fruit (page 100)
- Vanilla (page 122)

Amaze Your Family and Friends

These plants make you say wow! They are not the simplest to grow, but with a little attention to care and culture, they'll produce remarkable fruit that will win over even the most skeptical guest.

- Black pepper (page 116)
- 'Buddha's Hand' citron (page 22)
- Lemon (page 30)
- Miracle berry (page 74)
- Peanut butter fruit (page 90)
- Sapodilla (page 98)
- Sweet lemon (page 42)

RIGHT: A fruiting tree is an elegant, colorful accent in a sunny living room.

kumquat

myrtle-leaf orange

grapefruit

'Buddha's Hand' citron

1
Citrus Fruits

Citron · Citrumelo
Grapefruit · Kumquat
Lemons · Limes
Oranges · Sunquat · Tangerine

Australian Finger Lime

Citrus australasica

SIT-rus aw-strah-LAY-see-kuh

Plant Particulars

Size and form
2–3 feet with pruning; shrub

Bloom season
Year-round

Fruiting season
Year-round

Family
Rutaceae

Origin
Australia

Australian finger lime is one of the easiest citrus to grow and gets an A+ for its ornamental quality. Best of all, it bears small, tapered yellowish green fruits that are a treat unto themselves. Once the fruit is mature, simply slice a finger lime open and prepare to be delightfully surprised. Unique to Australian finger lime, hundreds of tiny individual juice beads (technically called vesicles) are packed inside the fruit. These burst open when you eat them, filling your mouth with a pleasantly sour lime flavor. We use Australian finger lime as a garnish or in beverages. (See Logee's Australian Finger "Lime-Aid" on page 19.)

Australian finger lime has a resilient root system and tolerates dryness in both the soil and atmosphere. Plants need to reach a foot or more in height and fill out a 6-inch pot before they will bear heavily. After that, several flowering and fruiting cycles occur each year, so they become constant producers over time.

*A note of caution: Thorny spikes, much like those of a rose, are prevalent.

Varieties We grow two forms of Australian finger lime. The species itself has an upright growth habit; its leaves are no more than ¼ inch long. With its dense stems and ability to withstand dryness, it makes an excellent bonsai subject. The second form, a hybrid between *C. australasica* and an unknown parent, has a spreading and mounding habit and leaves about 1 inch long. Its fruits are seedless. Both the species and the hybrid bear small white flowers with little fragrance.

Australian finger lime

Recipes from the Tropical Kitchen

Logee's Australian Finger "Lime-Aid"

Shawn Detoro, Logee's customer service representative, created this drink for one of our management meetings. It was a hot summer's day, the air was stagnant, and everyone was thirsty. After drinking Shawn's lime-aid, we had a burst of creative energy. We don't know if it was the little vesicles of sour juice exploding in our mouths or the sugar high that sparked us, but whatever it was, we recommend this beverage whenever you need a shot of inspiration.

1	cup organic sugar
4–5	cups water
1	cup fresh lime juice (6–8 fresh limes; Key limes or Persian limes are best)
6–8	Australian finger limes

Make a simple syrup by bringing the sugar and 1 cup water to a boil in a small saucepan over high heat. Let cool to room temperature. In a large pitcher, combine the simple syrup and lime juice. Add 3 cups cold water and taste. Add more water to taste. Refrigerate for 30–40 minutes. Place ice in six tall, clear glasses, along with a straw or stirrer. Cut the Australian finger limes into quarters. Using the rim of a glass, scoop the beads of lime into the glasses. Pour in the juice mixture, stir, and serve.

Serves 6

Growing Conditions

Light: Full sun

Soil: Well-drained potting mix

Minimum indoor temperature: 35°F (2°C)

Hardiness outdoors: Zone 9

Care

Fertilizing: Moderate feeder; feed weekly or every other week throughout the growing season or when temperatures are above 60°F (15°C). Reduce or stop during winter.

Pruning: Prune anytime growth is excessive, but prune selectively. Do not head back the entire plant at once, because flower buds form on hardened growth from the previous year. Be sure to leave some year-old growth intact to bear flowers and fruit.

Potential Problems

Pests: Scale and mealybugs

Foliar disease: Not susceptible

Root disease: Not susceptible; strong root system

Scoop out the juice-filled vesicles from inside the fruit to garnish a salad or add a tangy touch to beverages.

TOP RIGHT: Australian finger lime bears flowers and fruit year-round

19

Calamondin Orange

× *Citrofortunella mitis*

ex sit-roh-for-toon-NEL-uh MIT-iss

For generations, calamondin orange has been one of the best-known and best-loved potted citrus. The name *calamondin* is derived from the common name of this plant in the Philippines, where it is also called *agridulce*, meaning sweet and sour. It grows well on a windowsill and produces an abundance of tiny sour oranges. These can be used like lemons or limes in baking or beverages, and they make an excellent marmalade. The popularity of this fruit spans the globe; in Southeast Asia, almost every home has a calamondin orange.

Some say that a calamondin is a cross between a kumquat and a mandarin orange. Others claim it is a cross between a lime and a mandarin orange or a lime and a kumquat. Whatever the true parentage, calamondin has a bushy growth habit that is easily pruned to maintain a small but full specimen. It is often used for bonsai because it is easy to maintain as a small plant. The highly fragrant blossoms and ornamental appeal of tiny oranges that remain on plants year-round endear calamondin orange even to gardeners who have never considered growing citrus. Variegated calamondin orange is a new twist, adding mottled green and cream-colored leaves and striped fruit.

Plant Particulars

Size and form
2–3 feet with pruning; bushy miniature tree

Bloom season
Year-round; heaviest from late winter into summer

Fruiting season
Year-round

Family
Rutaceae

Origin
Thought to be China

Calamondin orange

Calamondin Orange Marmalade

Our calamondin orange tree at Logee's greenhouses has been growing in the same spot for almost 60 years and bears oranges about the size of a lime year-round. Our customer service supervisor, Ashley Ravenelle, collected the oranges and found out that they needed to be refrigerated once picked, or else they would mold. After lots of experimentation, this delicious marmalade recipe evolved. Try it as a gourmet accoutrement to meat or fish or a simple topping on toast or scones.

calamondin oranges (enough to generate approximately 3 cups purée)

3 cups organic sugar

¼ cup water

Cut the calamondin oranges in half and remove all seeds, but not the peels. Place in a food processor and purée. Measure, then transfer to a heavy, nonstick saucepan. If you end up with more or less than 3 cups of purée, adjust the sugar accordingly. Add the sugar and water to the saucepan. Bring to a boil and simmer for approximately 30 minutes, stirring frequently to avoid burning. Pour into sterilized half-pint jars. Let cool and refrigerate. For long-term storage, process in a boiling water bath as you would regular marmalade.

Makes 4 to 6 half-pint jars

Growing Conditions

Light: Full sun

Soil: Well-drained potting mix

Minimum indoor temperature: 60°F (15°C) for active growth; will tolerate temperatures into the 30s (−1 to 4°C)

Hardiness outdoors: Zone 8

Care

Fertilizing: Moderate amounts of fertilizer weekly during active growth. Discontinue in winter and under cool conditions.

Pruning: Pinch and prune young plants to encourage branching. After that, prune anytime growth is excessive to maintain form and size. For the least disturbance to next season's fruit, prune mature plants after fruit has set.

Potential Problems

Pests: Some susceptibility to scale and mealybugs

Foliar disease: Few problems

Root disease: Susceptible, especially in cool and wet conditions

× *Citrofortunella mitis*

Tiny new fruits, full-size oranges, and white flowers all appear simultaneously on calamondin plants.

TOP RIGHT: Fruits of the variegated variety start out with green and yellow variegation but turn orange when ripe.

Citron

Citrus medica

SIT-rus MED-ee-kuh

One of the oldest known citrus in cultivation, citrons date back to the Babylonian civilizations of 6000 BC. They are vigorous plants that bear easily and have an upright, open growth habit. They flower throughout the year, although, like other citrus, spring and summer is the heaviest blooming time. Citron has a reputation for being short-lived if planted in the ground, but when grown as a container plant it can survive for years. Root disease can be a problem. To prevent it, give plants plenty of warmth, and water carefully to avoid overly moist soil conditions.

'Buddha's Hand' has large fingerlike protrusions on its fruits, which can develop as open fingers or a closed hand, depending on the time of year and environmental conditions. As often as we've grown 'Buddha's Hand', we're unable to predict which shape the "hand" will grow into. The medium-sized fruits consist of a solid, heavy, sweet rind with no pulp or seeds inside. In Asia, tradition has it that anyone who possesses 'Buddha's Hand' will have a long life of happiness.

'Etrog' has significance to people of the Jewish faith. During the Feast of Tabernacles (Sukkot), an *etrog* (Hebrew for citron), symbolizing the fruit of the Promised Land, is carried to the temple. These fruits have sour pulp and seeds at the center, but the surrounding white flesh is sweet. The flesh is 2–3 inches thick; the yellow outer rind is paper-thin.

'Turunj' produces oversize fruit. We once picked a 'Turunj' from one of the trees at Logee's greenhouses that weighed more than 7 pounds, measured 14 inches long, and was shaped like a giant football. Because 'Turunj' fruits can grow so large, it's essential to train young plants to develop thick, dense branches. You'll also need to provide support for branches of young mature plants so they won't break under the weight of the fruit. Older mature plants can hold the fruit without support.

Plant Particulars

Size and form
3–5 feet with pruning; upright tree

Bloom season
Intermittently year-round

Fruiting season
Intermittently year-round

Family
Rutaceae

Origin
Unknown; first cultivated in the Middle East and Persia (Iran)

'Buddha's Hand' citron

This seven-and-a-half-pound 'Turunj' fruit grew on a plant that was only 4 feet tall.

BELOW LEFT: 'Etrog' citrons yield abundant sweet pulp that has a texture similar to apple flesh.

BELOW RIGHT: 'Buddha's Hand' citrons could serve as Halloween decorations with their weird handlike appearance.

Interior of an 'Etrog' citron

Growing Conditions

Light: Full sun

Soil: Well-drained potting mix

Minimum indoor temperature: 60°F (15°C)

Hardiness outdoors: Zone 9; needs protection from frost

Care

Fertilizing: Feed with a balanced fertilizer weekly or every other week throughout the growing season. Discontinue in winter.

Pruning: Pinch and prune young plants to encourage branching. After flowering and fruit set, prune anytime growth is excessive. 'Buddha's Hand' tends to develop long branches. Head these back to encourage lower lateral branching, which will be stronger for holding fruit.

Potential Problems

Pests: Scale and mealybugs; spider mites in dry conditions

Foliar disease: Few problems

Root disease: Susceptible in wet and cool conditions

Citrumelo

Citrus × paradisi × Ponciris trifoliata

SIT-rus ex par-ah-DEE-see ex pon-SYE-rus try-foe-lee-AY-tuh

Citrumelo, also called hardy grapefruit, is famous for its indestructible root system. Most other citrus have some susceptibility to root disease, but the roots of this hybrid are disease-free in containers. Because of this quality, it's also used as an understock for other citrus. Another reason to try citrumelo is its cold tolerance: plants can survive temperatures down into the teens for short periods. The original citrumelo plant in our greenhouses came from an unheated greenhouse in Newport, Rhode Island, and it grows quite happily in the North.

Citrumelo is a cross between a grapefruit and a hardy orange (*Poncirus trifoliata*). The fruits are sour and somewhat similar to an unripe grapefruit, with the slight bitter aftertaste carried over from its *Poncirus* parent. On mature trees, fruits can become quite large and ripen to an orange color. Plants are often grown from seed and can take up to seven years to fruit and flower. Plants grown from cuttings will flower within a year and will bear shortly thereafter. Compared to other types of grapefruit, citrumelo remains modest in size, whether planted in a pot or in the ground. The cultivar that we grow confers a dwarfing effect when used as a rootstock for other citrus.

Plant Particulars

Size and form
4–6 feet with pruning; upright tree

Bloom season
Late winter to early spring

Fruiting season
Late fall and winter

Family
Rutaceae

Origin
Hybridized in the United States

Citrumelo

Surprisingly, hardy grapefruits turn orange as they ripen

RIGHT: This young citrus plant is grafted on a Citrumelo roostock, chosen because of its resilience.

BOTTOM RIGHT: A ripe citrumelo

Growing Conditions

Light: Full sun

Soil: Well-drained potting mix

Minimum indoor temperature: 35°F (2°C); can tolerate temperatures as low as 10°F (−12°C) for short periods

Hardiness outdoors: Zone 7

Care

Fertilizing: Moderate feeders; fertilize weekly or every other week from spring to fall, and discontinue in the winter.

Pruning: Prune after fruit set or whenever needed to maintain form.

Potential Problems

Pests: Scale and mealybugs; spider mites under hot, dry conditions

Foliar disease: Not susceptible

Root disease: Not susceptible

Grapefruit

Citrus × paradisi

SIT-rus ex par-ah-DEE-see

Grapefruits are surprisingly good container plants that are easy to grow in pots and have a full yet contained form. The flowers are highly fragrant, and if given full sun, the plants bloom and bear reliably every year. The fruits offer ornamental appeal and hold well on the tree for months while ripening. They become quite large, so young trees will carry only a few fruits.

It's important to shape young plants to encourage lateral branching. Plants need this strong branch structure in order to support the often heavy weight of the grapefruits.

'Ruby Red' is one of the oldest pink-fleshed varieties, famous for its sweet, juicy, pink-blushed pulp. It is widely grown by commercial orchardists, and 'Ruby Red' grapefruits are a popular feature in grocery store produce displays.

'Golden Grapefruit' is a rare cultivar with orange flesh. Its sweetness comes from its orange lineage, which makes it slightly less acid than white or pink varieties. 'Golden Grapefruit' bears reliably every year in containers. Mature plants can produce an abundance of fruit.

Plant Particulars

Size and form
3–5 feet with pruning; upright tree

Bloom season
Late winter and spring

Fruiting season
Fall and winter

Family
Rutaceae

Origin
Caribbean Islands

Grapefruit

Recipes from the Tropical Kitchen

Pink Grapefruit Granita

This simple recipe is refreshing and delightful, perfect after a heavy meal.

1   cup organic sugar
1   cup water
4   cups fresh pink grapefruit juice
1   tablespoon finely grated pink
     grapefruit zest

In a small saucepan, make a simple syrup by heating the sugar and water until just boiling, then let cool. Add the juice and zest, and stir.

Pour the mixture into a 2- or 4-quart pan and place in the freezer, stirring every 30 minutes for 2 to 3 hours to encourage crystals to form. Serve immediately. If you forget to stir and your mixture becomes solid, salvage it by scraping the surface with a fork.

Serves 8

Unlike oranges, grapefruits don't become pithy inside, even when left on the tree after ripening.

TOP RIGHT: 'Golden Grapefruit' has unusual orange pulp.

Growing Conditions

Light: Full sun

Soil: Well-drained potting mix

Minimum indoor temperature: 50°F (10°C); can withstand temperatures down to freezing for short periods

Hardiness outdoors: Zone 9

Care

Fertilizing: Moderate fertilizer during the growing season. Discontinue in fall and winter, especially if nighttime temperatures are consistently below 60°F (15°C). Iron chlorosis can develop, especially during winter when growth is slow and soil is cool. (See page 132).

Pruning: Prune in spring after flowering is complete. Spring and summer growth creates the buds that will produce flowers the following year.

Potential Problems

Pests: Scale and mealybugs; spider mites in dry, warm conditions

Foliar disease: Not susceptible

Root disease: Highly susceptible, especially during periods of low light and cool, wet soils

Kumquat

Fortunella species and cultivars

for-toon-NEL-uh

𝕂umquats are little orange jewels of tasty delight. The fruit is entirely edible, even the skin. Simply pop a kumquat, about the size of a large grape, into your mouth. Depending on the variety, an intense flavor from tangy to sour to deliciously sweet will explode on your tongue.

In general, kumquats make excellent container plants. They are heavy producers that flower and fruit reliably, often as young plants. (We have seen young kumquats in 2½-inch pots setting fruit!) Generally, they are grown as grafted plants. With the correct understock (such as citrumelo or *Citrus macrophylla*), they can be resistant to root disease. The flowers are highly fragrant and the plants bloom abundantly, filling a room with heavy citrus fragrance. The fruits ripen in early winter and cling on the trees until late spring.

Fortunella margarita 'Nagami', also known as oval kumquat, is the most popular and the one usually found in the produce section of grocery stores. Fruits are oval with an outer sweet skin and sour center.

F. crassifolia 'Meiwa' is also called sweet kumquat. Its round fruits have candylike sweetness in both skin and pulp; it is the best one for eating out of hand. 'Meiwa' tends to drop its leaves as the fruits develop and ripen. This characteristic creates a thin-looking specimen, but it will fill out with new leaves again once the fruit is harvested.

F. obovata 'Fukushu', the Changshou kumquat, has a flavor that is somewhere between the other two varieties, with a sweet skin and slightly tart center. 'Fukushu' is an obscure variety in North America but is often grown in China as a potted plant. The pear-shaped fruit is larger than that of 'Meiwa' or 'Nagami'. Young trees produce fruit abundantly and can bear twice a year. If we could grow only one kumquat, it would be 'Fukushu'.

Plant Particulars

Size and form
3–5 feet with pruning; upright tree

Bloom season
Generally summer

Fruiting season
Winter into summer

Family name
Rutaceae

Origin
China

'Nagami' kumquat

Sweet flavor and a nearly perfect round shape make 'Meiwa' a highly desirable kumquat.

RIGHT: 'Fukushu' bears fruits as large as apples and much sweeter than those of other kumquat varieties.

Growing Conditions

Light: Full sun

Soil: Well-drained potting mix

Minimum indoor temperature: 35°F (2°C)

Hardiness outdoors: Zone 8

Care

Fertilizing: Moderate feeders; fertilize weekly or every other week from late spring into fall, and discontinue in winter.

Pruning: Once fruit is set, plants can be pruned to make full bushy specimens or standards.

Potential Problems

Pests: Scale and mealybugs

Foliar disease: Not susceptible

Root disease: Susceptible if not grafted onto a disease-resistant rootstock

'Nagami' kumquat

Martha Stewart's Kumquat Pick

When we took Martha Stewart on a tour of our greenhouses, she marveled at our 9-foot-tall 150-year-old kumquat tree, which had grown out of its pot and rooted itself in the aisle. The base of the tree's trunk has the shape of a 12-inch pot. The pot is long gone, but the tree continues to produce eight different varieties of citrus, all grafted on the one tree. We picked and tasted the 'Meiwa' kumquat and the 'Nagami' kumquat. We thought Martha would prefer the 'Meiwa' hands down, but she proclaimed the 'Nagami', with all its sour tartness, by far the best-tasting kumquat ever.

Lemon

Citrus limon

SIT-rus LEE-mun

We recommend that every household, especially those inclined toward culinary delight, grow its own lemon tree. At Logee's greenhouses, the lemon trees are covered with ripe lemons every fall. And because the greenhouse where we keep our mother plants is so full of big plants, we now grow most of our lemon trees in hanging baskets. Heat rises, of course, and the trees love the warmth near the top of the greenhouse. We're always amazed by the sheer number of fruit they produce. It's not unusual for a tree growing in a 12-inch basket to bear 30 or more lemons.

In general, lemons are easy to care for and fast growing. The fruits can be left on the tree to harvest throughout the year.

'Meyer' lemon is famous for its essence, flavor, and many uses; it's like having an old friend in the kitchen. Plants will grow almost continuously under warm conditions and high light; therefore, the upright, spreading branches need to be pruned back to maintain a dense, well-branched specimen. Prune young plants to create strong scaffolding that will bear the weight of plentiful fruits when the plant matures. 'Meyer' is thought to be a hybrid between a lemon and a sour orange. It will produce almost twice as much juice as the common table lemon and has a distinct rich flavor.

'Ponderosa' is extremely vigorous and bears fruit easily. The fruits are strong, flavorful, and quite acid, making them great for baking and cooking. Since each fruit of a 'Ponderosa' is large, sometimes reaching up to 5 pounds, pay special attention to shaping the young plant to create a full, well-branched specimen able to hold the heavy weight. Limbs left unpruned may tear under the strain of the heavy fruits. 'Ponderosa' is a hybrid between a lemon and citron (see page 22).

table

Plant Particulars

Size and form
3–5 feet with pruning; upright tree or shrub

Bloom season
Intermittently year-round, but mainly late winter to spring

Fruiting season
Generally fall, but also late winter and spring

Family
Rutaceae

Origin
Asia

'Meyer' lemon

'Meyer' lemon blossoms show a lavender blush when closed, but petals unfurl as pearly white. When you pick a 'Meyer' fruit, notice the delicious lemon scent that escapes from the stem end.

TOP RIGHT: A lemon-yellow rind masks the pink pulp inside this 'Spanish Pink Variegata' lemon.

'Spanish Pink Variegata' is a showpiece that's well worth growing for its variegated foliage, striped fruit, and pink pulp. The green to light green, striped fruit turns pink to yellow when ripe. This variety fruits easily, and the juice is comparable to that of a common table lemon. The only challenge is its uncompromising open growth habit. Pruning regularly when a plant is young is essential to promote dense, bushy growth; without rigorous pruning, the plants will end up with a loose and scraggly form.

Growing Conditions

Light: Full sun

Soil: Well-drained potting mix

Minimum indoor temperature: 50°F (10°C); 'Meyer' prefers temperatures above 65°F (18°C). When temperatures dip lower, reduce watering and fertilization to minimize chance of root rot.

Hardiness outdoors: Zone 9; protect from frost, with the exception of 'Meyer', which can tolerate brief exposure to temperatures into the high 20s (−4 to −2°C)

Care

Fertilizing: Moderate feeder; fertilize weekly or every other week throughout the active growing season as long as temperatures are warm. Reduce or stop in winter.

Pruning: Prune at any time of the year. For the least disruption to fruiting, wait until the spring flush of flowering is complete to head back plants to maintain form and size.

Potential Problems

Pests: Scale and mealybugs; spider mites under hot, dry conditions

Foliar disease: Not susceptible

Root disease: Highly susceptible, especially in cool, wet soils and under low light

This 'Ponderosa' lemon tree arrived at Logee's greenhouses by horse and buggy a century ago. It's been planted in the same spot ever since, growing so large that we call this spot "The Lemon Tree House." The tree bears fruits that weigh up to 5 pounds apiece. Plus, we harvest thousands of cuttings from the tree every year.

Recipes from the Tropical Kitchen

Ponderosa Lemon Bread

Joy Logee Martin (Byron's mother) loved her lemons but even more so she loved this lemon bread that Barbara Glass (Laurelynn's mother) made for her every Christmas. Excellent with afternoon tea.

Cake

6	tablespoons butter
1	cup sugar
1	teaspoon grated zest of 'Ponderosa' lemon
3	tablespoons juice of 'Ponderosa' lemon
2	large eggs, beaten
1 ½	cups all-purpose flour
1	teaspoon baking powder
½	teaspoon salt
½	cup milk

Glaze

½	cup fresh 'Ponderosa' lemon juice
½	cup sugar

Preheat the oven to 350°F. Grease an 8- by 4½-inch loaf pan. Cream the butter and sugar together. Add the lemon zest, lemon juice, and eggs. Combine the flour, baking powder, and salt and add to the creamed mixture, alternating with the milk. Pour into the prepared pan and bake for 50 minutes.

While the cake is baking, prepare the glaze. Combine the juice and sugar and mix until the sugar dissolves.

When the cake is done and removed from the oven, spoon the glaze over the cake (while it is still in the pan). Let it stand until the glaze is absorbed. Cool and serve in ½-inch slices.

Makes approximately 14 to 16 slices

Logee's Meyer Lemonade with a Hint of Lime

Napa Howe, our lead grower at Logee's, and his girlfriend, Laura Beausoleil, have been enjoying their special version of Logee's Meyer Lemonade for the past two summers. The staff loves it so much that they drink it year-round. This recipe calls for only two 'Meyer' lemons to make 32 ounces of lemonade because each 'Meyer' lemon is packed with fresh juice. We especially like the combination of 'Meyer' lemon with the oily juice of a kaffir lime, but any kind of fresh lime juice can be used.

½	cup organic sugar
4	cups water
½	cup 'Meyer' lemon juice, strained (about 2 ripe lemons)
4	teaspoons fresh lime juice, strained (about 1 lime)

Make a simple syrup by combining the sugar and ½ cup water in a saucepan over high heat. Bring to a boil, stir to dissolve, then cool. In a large pitcher, combine the simple syrup, remaining 3½ cups water, and lemon and lime juice. Stir and enjoy.

Serves 4 to 6

Evening Adult Treat

If you dare, try a "Logee's Meyer Margarita" by mixing ⅔ cup of Logee's Meyer Lemonade with ice and ½ ounce of your favorite tequila. Strain into a margarita glass over a curly zest from a 'Meyer' lemon.

Lime

Citrus aurantifolia

SIT-rus aw-ran-tih-FOH-lee-uh

You'll have three choices of limes for growing in containers. Key limes pack a powerful flavor punch for their size. Persian lime is milder than Key lime, while sweet Palestine lime really is sweet and lacks the acidity that's typical of citrus fruits. Most people don't know that limes actually turn yellow when they ripen, and therefore, a true Key lime pie is yellow, not green.

When growing limes, pay special attention to avoid overwatering, because all types are susceptible to root diseases.

Key lime, also known as Mexican lime, is famous for its culinary uses, especially Key lime pie. This plant is an excellent choice for container culture, producing edible fruits over a long period. Flowering is heaviest in late winter, but a Key lime plant can flower and fruit at any time of the year. Its small leaves and densely branching habit are a plus for gardeners with limited growing space. Amazingly enough, a Key lime plant can be kept less than 2 feet tall and still produce an abundance of fruit. With good culture, it will cover itself in small limes that eventually ripen to yellow. One of the few truly tropical (as opposed to subtropical) citrus, Key limes grow best above 60°F (15°C) and preferably above 65°F (18°C).

Persian lime is a more open and robust plant that produces larger, seedless fruits, with fewer fruits per plant. This vigorous variety needs more space to grow than Key lime. For best production in a container, allow for at least a 3- to 4-foot spread.

Sweet Palestine lime puts more energy into flowering and fruiting than growing taller, making it an outstanding plant for container culture. This variety flowers throughout the year, and fruit ripens on a continual basis. Sweet Palestine lime is a bit more prone to root diseases; for best results grow it in clay pots, avoid temperatures below 60°F (15°C), and allow the soil to dry out between waterings. The fruits, about the size of a standard lime, have sweet pulp with a slight insipid aftertaste. When grown in cool winter temperatures, the fruits ripen sweeter with little if any aftertaste.

Plant Particulars

Size and form
2–4 feet with pruning; bushy shrub

Bloom season
Generally late winter or early spring, but can flower year-round

Fruiting season
Fall into winter, although fruit can ripen year-round

Family
Rutaceae

Origin
East Indies and Polynesia

Persian lime

Palestine and Key Lime Mojito

Nicole Lessard, Logee's graphic designer, has an eye for flair, color, and placement, so we knew that Nicole's mojitos, featured at her "Girls' Day" get-together, would be a hit. And they were! She served the mojitos in mason jars, along with finger sandwiches and dessert. What a treat.

¾ cup fresh sweet Palestine lime juice
¾ cup fresh Key lime juice
2 ½ cups light rum
¾–1 cup confectioners' sugar
¾–1 cup club soda (or raspberry-lime seltzer)
10 large sprigs fresh mint (4–6 leaves per sprig)
Crushed ice
Key lime wedges, for garnish

In a large pitcher, combine the lime juices, rum, and sugar. Stir until the sugar has dissolved. Stir in the club soda. Place mint sprigs in each of ten glasses. Using the back of a spoon, crush the mint leaves. Add crushed ice to the glasses. Divide the rum mixture among the glasses. Garnish with lime wedges. Serve immediately.

Serves 10

Growing Conditions

Light: Full sun

Soil: Well-drained potting mix

Minimum indoor temperature: Persian and sweet Palestine limes, 50°F (10°C); will tolerate temperatures down to freezing for short periods. Key lime needs temperatures above 60°F (15°C).

Hardiness outdoors: Persian and sweet Palestine limes, Zone 9; Key lime, Zone 10

Care

Fertilizing: Moderate fertilizer during the growing season. Discontinue in fall and winter, especially if nighttime temperatures are consistently below 60°F (15°C).

Pruning: Persian lime needs pinching and pruning when young to encourage branching and thus increase fruiting. To maintain all types of lime plants at the desired height, head back branches right after harvest. Pruning at other times can reduce fruit production.

Potential Problems

Pests: Scale and mealybugs; spider mites when under hot, dry conditions (common indoors during winter)

Foliar disease: Not susceptible

Root disease: Highly susceptible, especially during the winter

All limes change from green to yellow when ripe. Key lime fruits (shown here) are smaller than those of Persian limes (top right).

Myrtle-Leaf Orange

Citrus myrtifolia

SIT-rus mir-tih-FOH-lee-uh

Plant Particulars

Size and form
2–4 feet with pruning; upright tree

Bloom season
Late winter and spring, but can flower into summer

Fruiting season
Late fall and winter; ripe fruit hangs on tree for months

Family
Rutaceae

Origin
China

Myrtle-leaf orange is highly regarded as an ornamental. Even when ripe, its small oranges hold on the branches for months, and its compact nature makes it prized as a windowsill plant. Myrtle-leaf orange (also called Chinotto orange) withstands dry soil well, and it's an ideal candidate for bonsai culture, with its gnarly, twisted woody stems. When mature, its highly fragrant white flowers, dense myrtlelike leaves, and long fruiting season make this a showpiece worthy of a photo spread in *Martha Stewart Living* magazine. The sour fruits are not often eaten fresh but can be candied or used in preserves and jellies.

We acquired our first myrtle-leaf orange in the 1970s from Uncle Richard Logee. We maintained the specimen in a 12-inch pot for years. The trunk thickened to 3 inches wide, and the plant covered itself in flowers and fruit every year. We still have this plant today.

Fruiting is heavy even on small plants. For a limited space or if bonsai culture is desired, keep the roots cramped in a small pot. Typically growing a myrtle-leaf orange in a 4- to 6-inch pot will force the stems to become woody and twisted while still flowering and fruiting. Under these conditions, you can prune plants to remain less than 16 inches tall. Even as a floor specimen, myrtle-leaf orange can be maintained at less than 3 feet tall. The most important cultural requirement other than sunlight is managing soil moisture. Always grow on the dry side to avoid root rot, which often develops if the potting mix remains cool and wet.

Myrtle-leaf orange

Miniature bright orange fruits decorate the branches of myrtle-leaf orange for months on end.

TOP RIGHT: Fragrant blossoms are another attraction of this delightful citrus-family member.

Growing Conditions

Light: Full sun

Soil: Well-drained potting mix

Minimum indoor temperature: 50°F (10°C)

Hardiness outdoors: Zone 8

Care

Fertilizing: Moderate fertilizer during the growing season. Discontinue in fall and winter, especially if nighttime temperatures are consistently below 60°F (15°C).

Pruning: Prune after flowering as needed to control size. This timing allows the new growth to mature and form buds for next year's flowers.

Potential Problems

Pests: Mealybugs and scale

Foliar disease: Few problems

Root disease: Highly susceptible when grown in wet, cool conditions

 **Experimenting with Bonsai**

Myrtle-leaf orange is a great choice for a bonsai project because its growth habit has a tight structure, it can be kept in a small container for years, and it holds its leaves well even when under drought stress. It's also easy to prune a myrtle-leaf orange plant to maintain shape and form.

To start, you'll need to decide on a form for your bonsai, which can be twisted or bent. For example, if you decide on a bent form, start by potting up the myrtle-leaf orange so that its main stem is at an angle to the container rather than perpendicular to it. As the main stem grows, you'll use wire to direct the plant's growth on that same angle rather than allowing it to grow straight up.

Orange

Citrus sinensis

SIT-rus sye-NEN-sis

Oranges are rewarding potted plants and a great source of entertainment for gardeners of all ages. They are slower growing than other members of the citrus tribe, but if given time they will form shapely specimens. Success in growing the sweet edible oranges depends on maintaining a healthy root system and giving the plants a bright sunny spot. The navels, known for easy peeling and seedless fruit, usually ripen around November and December; if grown in pots they may bear fruit only every other year.

'Tiger Navel' is variegated and consistently produces sweet fruits. Unlike other navels, this cultivar has excellent fruit-holding capacity, with oranges often hanging on into the spring. The foliage is beautifully marbled and striped in tones of green and white.

'Sanguinelli' or blood orange consistently fruits and holds well on the tree. Its purple-red flesh and crisp, sparkling flavor are enhanced by cool temperatures (the high 30s to the 40s [3–9°C]) during fruit formation and ripening. It bears reliably every year, but under warm conditions indoors, the purple pigmentation may not be uniform.

'Valencia' is the most widely planted edible citrus in the world. Its sweet and seedless fruits, ability to hold on the tree, and constant production make 'Valencia' highly desirable for both producers and consumers. These same qualities give 'Valencia' an advantage over other citrus as a container plant. Unlike most other oranges, its fruit ripens in the spring and early summer.

Plant Particulars

Size and form
3–5 feet with pruning; upright tree

Bloom season
Late winter and spring

Fruiting season
Most types in fall and winter

Family
Rutaceae

Origin
Southeast Asia

Orange

ABOVE AND BELOW RIGHT: Ripe 'Valencia' oranges are a treat in spring and early summer.

LEFT: 'Tiger Navel' fruits are highly ornamental, and they last well on the tree even when ripe.

TOP RIGHT: Although they look ordinary on the outside, 'Sanguinelli' fruits have purple-red flesh inside.

Growing Conditions

Light: Full sun

Soil: Well-drained potting mix

Minimum indoor temperature: 50°F (10°C); warm temperatures in winter will help keep roots healthy

Hardiness outdoors: Zone 9

Care

Fertilizing: Moderate feed during the growing season; use a balanced fertilizer with trace minerals. Discontinue in fall and winter, especially if nighttime temperatures are consistently below 60°F (15°C). Iron chlorosis can be a problem, especially during winter when growth is slow and soil is cool. (See page 132.)

Pruning: Prune after flowering is complete; spring and summer growth creates the flowers for the next season. For varieties such as navels that bear every other year, do not prune during an off year, or else flowering can be disrupted.

Potential Problems

Pests: Scale and mealybugs; spider mites in dry, warm indoor conditions

Foliar disease: Not susceptible

Root disease: Highly susceptible, especially during periods of low light and cool, wet soils

39

Sunquat

× *Citrofortunella* 'Sunquat'

ex sit-roh-for-toon-NEL-lah SUN-kwat

Perfectly designed for container culture, 'Sunquat' is hard to beat. It combines the heavy blooming and fruiting characteristics of kumquats with the everbearing characteristic of lemons. Surprisingly, this cultivar will flower more than it will grow. The highly fragrant flowers mimic kumquat flowers and keep coming all year.

We gave a ripe sunquat fruit to our children and encouraged them to take a bite, rind and all. Biting into what looked like a pale yellow lemon surprised their taste buds with a sweet orangey flavor. The entire fruit can be eaten just like an apple; it has a sweet rind and a juicy, tangy-sweet pulp.

Sunquat plants have an irregular form, but luckily their heavy branches easily carry an abundance of fruit with little trouble. Plants that are propagated from cuttings start bearing fruit within a year of their initial cutting. With heavy pruning they can be maintained at less than 2 feet tall. Another irregularity is the size of the fruits. On the same plant, some can be as large as a medium-sized orange while other fruits are as small as a calamondin orange. For the greatest sweetness, leave fruit on the tree until it is fully ripe. To test, try lightly touching a fruit. If it falls off, it's ready!

Plant Particulars

Size and form
2–3 feet with pruning; upright tree

Bloom season
Year-round

Fruiting season
Year-round

Family
Rutaceae

Origin
Texas; chance seedling thought to be a cross between a lemon and a 'Meiwa' kumquat

'Sunquat'

A 'Sunquat' plant produces fruit in various sizes, depending on the size of the branch.

Growing Conditions

Light: Full sun

Soil: Well-drained potting mix

Minimum indoor temperature: 60°F (15°C) for active growth; will tolerate temperatures into the 30s (−1 to 4°C) for short periods

Hardiness outdoors: Zone 9

Care

Fertilizing: Moderate amounts of fertilizer during active growth and when temperatures are above 60°F (15°C). In winter and under cool conditions, discontinue.

Pruning: Prune anytime growth is excessive. For the least disturbance to next season's flower buds, prune after fruit has set.

Potential Problems

Pests: Some susceptibility to scale and mealybugs; also to spider mites in hot, dry conditions

Foliar disease: Not susceptible

Root disease: Susceptible, especially when grown cool and wet

 # Know Your Lineage

We like to understand the parentage of the plants we grow because it offers clues on how to best care for the plants. 'Sunquat' is a good example. The 'Sunquat' is a cross between a kumquat and a lemon. The kumquat genetics contribute heavy bloom and intensely fragrant flowers. Heavy bloom means heavy fruit production, which often means that a plant will require structural support to prevent branches from breaking under the weight of all that fruit. However, the lemon parentage results in plants that have naturally strong branches but also an irregular form. Thus, rather than support, what 'Sunquat' plants really need is proper pruning when young to create the best possible structure in preparation for abundant fruit.

Another interesting quality of 'Sunquat' plants is the variability in fruit size, which could be nature's inherent way of balancing the overall weight of fruit with a branch's capacity to carry fruit without cracking or snapping off.

Sweet Lemon

Citrus ujukitsu

SIT-rus oo-joo-KEET-soo

Sweet lemon is a unique species from Japan that produces yellow pear-shaped fruits that sometimes grow as large as softballs. As its name implies, the fruit's white flesh is sweet, and it's also easy to peel, making it a great choice for fresh eating. Of course, if you can't quite get over the fact that you are eating a lemon straight up, try it as a basis for sweet lemonade or iced tea that won't need sugar (see the recipe on page 43).

Sweet lemon is a reliable producer of flowers and fruit once it has grown 2 feet tall. Fruits form at the ends of the branches. They hold well on the tree and remain juicy and flavorful. Like so many of the edible sweet citrus, the flowers are highly fragrant. A few flowers alone will fill a room with sweet perfume.

Some experts say that a sweet lemon is a cross between a mandarin orange and a grapefruit, which is technically a tangelo. The distinguishing feature is the yellow skin, which makes it look like a lemon. Others say this cross is simply a tangelo with yellow skin. But whatever its origin, we know that this peel-and-eat lemon is the best around for a tasty sweet treat. However, you won't find a sweet lemon in a school lunch box — unless, of course, you are in Japan.

Plant Particulars

Size and form
3–5 feet with pruning; upright, sprawling tree

Bloom season
Late winter and spring

Fruiting season
Winter into spring

Family
Rutaceae

Origin
Japan

Sweet lemon

Recipes from the Tropical Kitchen

Sweet Lemon Iced Tea sans Sucre (without sugar)

Logee's shipping supervisor, Sabina Adorno, and her crew wrap live plants for shipment with the greatest of care, so it's no wonder that when Sabina developed this recipe, she took great care to get it just right. Sweet iced tea without sugar seems like a contradiction. Sabina found that when she used sweet lemon (*C. ujukitsu*) in unsweetened iced tea, the sweetness and lemony flavor were enough to convince any iced tea drinkers that they had stumbled upon a truly delightful beverage.

5	teaspoons black tea leaves
1½	cups boiling water
2½	cups cold water
½	cup fresh sweet lemon juice
	Sweet lemon zest, for garnish

Put the tea leaves in a teapot. Pour in the boiling water and allow to steep for 3 to 5 minutes, depending on the desired strength. Pour the cold water into a pitcher. Strain the brewed tea into the pitcher with the cold water and discard the tea leaves. Stir in the lemon juice. Pour over ice in iced tea glasses, garnish with lemon zest, and serve.

Serves 4

Growing Conditions

Light: Full sun

Soil: Well-drained potting mix

Minimum indoor temperature: 50°F (10°C)

Hardiness outdoors: Zone 9

Care

Fertilizing: Moderate fertilizer during the growing season; discontinue in the fall and winter, especially if nighttime temperatures are consistently below 60°F (15°C). Iron chlorosis can be a problem, especially during winter when growth is slow and soil is cool. (See page 132.)

Pruning: Prune young plants to form a well-branched specimen. Once plants reach maturity, head back branches in late spring after fruit has set; this timing allows flower buds to form for the following season while maintaining a shapely plant.

Potential Problems

Pests: Scale and mealybugs

Foliar disease: Not susceptible

Root disease: Susceptible to root rot

A bright yellow rind creates the expectation that this fruit will be sour, but the white flesh inside this sweet lemon is refreshingly sweet!

Tahitian Orange

Citrus × limonia 'Otaheite'

SIT-rus ex lim-OH-nee-ah oh-tah-HIGH-tee

Tahitian orange, which is actually thought to be a sweet lime, is one of the best ornamental oranges for container culture. Tahitian orange plants are naturally dwarf and produce abundant bright orange-red fruits that can literally hold on for years. Flowering happens on and off throughout the year. The plant will bloom best if slightly potbound; keep it tight in its pot and you will be rewarded year-round with fragrance and flowers.

The leaves of Tahitian orange plants have a slightly pungent smell that is distinct from other citrus varieties. If there is ever a question about the identity of a young plant, the leaf fragrance will end all doubt. Tahitian orange has an insipid aftertaste, and most gardeners agree that it is best used as an ornamental only. The cultivar name 'Otaheite' comes from a past name for the island of Tahiti.

Plant Particulars

Size and form
2–3 feet; bushy shrub

Bloom season
Year-round

Fruiting season
Year-round

Family
Rutaceae

Origin
India

Tahitian orange

The pink-tinged buds and fragrant blooms of Tahitian orange often mingle on the branches with the ripe fruit.

Growing Conditions

Light: Full sun

Soil: Well-drained potting mix

Minimum indoor temperature: 50°F (10°C)

Hardiness outdoors: Zone 9

Care

Fertilizing: Moderate fertilizer during the growing season. Discontinue in the fall and winter, especially if nighttime temperatures are consistently below 60°F (15°C). Iron chlorosis can be a problem, especially during winter when growth is slow and soil is cool. (See page 132.)

Pruning: Prune after fruit has set or whenever plants need shaping.

Potential Problems

Pests: Scale and mealybugs; spider mites in hot and dry conditions

Foliar disease: Not susceptible

Root disease: Highly susceptible; grow it in a clay pot and keep dry between waterings to minimize problems

⊙→ Fruit That Holds On and On

The fruit of Tahitian orange plants has an amazing capacity to hold on the branch for a long time after ripening. There is a Tahitian orange in our greenhouses that is now completing its second year of hanging on. When the fruit first ripens it has one of the deepest reddish orange colors of any citrus. As time passes, the fruit remains bright unless grown in a humid setting. Our greenhouses are quite humid, and our two-year-old Tahitian orange has turned green because algae is growing on the surface of the fruit! Although the fruit has ornamental appeal, if you leave too much fruit holding on the branches of a young Tahitian orange plant, the plant itself will not grow. We suggest leaving only a handful of fruit on the tree — pick the rest. This will allow the plant to continue growing. Once it reaches a size that is suitable for your growing space, you can let the fruit hang on the branch for as long as you like. Remember, flowering and fruiting continue year-round, and new fruit will be forming even when mature fruit is still attached to the plant.

Tangerine

Citrus reticulata

SIT-rus reh-tick-yoo-LAY-tuh

The tangerine, also called mandarin orange, although a slow grower, produces sweet and easy-to-peel fruits that ripen during the darkest days of the year. Upright and sprawling, it needs pruning to keep it contained and shapely. Flowers form on the first flush of new growth in late winter or spring. In containers in the North, flowering may happen every other year depending on the environmental conditions. In the winter, leaves may yellow due to iron chlorosis (see page 132), but as long as the root system is healthy, this is just a cosmetic problem. The new growth in late winter will remedy this problem.

'Dancy', which ripens in December, is often called the Christmas tangerine. 'Dancy' is prized for its larger than normal, easy-to-peel fruits and ability to hold on the tree longer than other varieties. However, if left on the tree too long, fruits will become pithy and dry.

'Kishu Seedless' bears smaller fruits that ripen from December through February. Its sweet, seedless, easy-to-peel tangerines are a mainstay lunch-box item in our household. This cultivar is excellent for pots for its ability to produce and hold fruit even while young.

Plant Particulars

Size and form
3–4 feet with pruning; upright tree

Bloom season
Late winter through spring

Fruiting season
December and January

Family
Rutaceae

Origin
China and Japan

Tangerine

Growing Conditions

Light: Full sun

Soil: Well-drained potting mix

Minimum indoor temperature: 50°F (10°C); can tolerate temperatures into the 30s (−1 to 4°C), but when they're grown cool, keep plants on the dry side to help prevent root rot

Hardiness outdoors: Zone 8

Care

Fertilizing: Moderate feeders; fertilize every other week during active growth, and discontinue in winter.

Pruning: Prune right after flowering to allow these slow growers enough time to form flower buds for the next season.

Potential Problems

Pests: Scale and mealybugs

Foliar disease: Few problems

Root disease: Susceptible, especially when grown cool and wet

The skin of 'Dancy' tangerines puckers when the fruit are ripe. The loose skin makes them easy to peel.

TOP RIGHT: 'Kishu Seedless' tangerines are a great snack when you're on the go.

Temple Orange

Citrus × tangor

SIT-rus ex TAN-gor

Temple orange, a cross between an orange and a tangerine, is well known as a tangy-sweet eating orange. It is grown mainly for table fruit thanks to an easy-peeling skin and a flavor all its own, like a miniature burst of fiery orange-red sunshine. Its flesh and outer peel ripen and darken as days become shorter.

One thing we enjoy about Temple oranges is that the plants reflower in late spring and bear a small second crop of fruit. We love the Temple oranges that we harvest in the winter, but it's an extra-special pleasure to have another round of them to eat in June!

Temple orange makes an excellent potted plant. Similar to a tangerine, it is slow growing and bears highly fragrant flowers. Like most potted citrus, it can be maintained in a 12- to 14-inch pot indefinitely. If fruits are left on the trees too long, their pulp will become dry.

Temple orange was discovered in Jamaica in 1896 by a fruit buyer named Boyce. Boyce sent budwood from the tree he'd come across to several friends in Winter Park, Florida. Eventually, a budded tree was brought to the attention of W. C. Temple, who recommended this sweet and delicious fruit to a nursery owner. The owner of Buckeye Nurseries, H. E. Gillett, named the orange Temple and began propagating it. It was first offered for sale in 1919, but it wasn't until the 1940s that it reached the level of mass production. Today Temple orange is a mainstay of the table fruit industry.

Plant Particulars

Size and form
3–5 feet when pruned; upright, spreading tree

Bloom season
Late winter to early spring; often reblooms in late spring

Fruiting season
Winter, sometimes with a second crop in early summer

Family
Rutaceae

Origin
Jamaica

Temple orange

Brightly colored Temple oranges are easy to peel.

RIGHT: Temple oranges can produce fruit twice a year. In our opinion, they are the best-tasting oranges around.

 ## Remember the Roots

Growing potted citrus is easy, but the plants can be prone to root disease, so it's very important to keep the roots healthy. Here's how:

- Avoid overpotting
- Use clay pots
- Avoid overfertilizing
- Wait to water until the soil is dry or plants show signs of drought stress
- Keep the soil warm

If your plants should develop root disease, don't despair! They will probably return to normal vigor once you change the environmental conditions.

Growing Conditions

Light: Full sun

Soil: Well-drained potting mix

Minimum indoor temperature: 50°F (10°C)

Hardiness outdoors: Zone 9

Care

Fertilizing: Fertilize weekly or every other week during the active growing season as long as temperatures are warm. Reduce or stop in winter.

Pruning: Selective pruning is needed when the plant is young to counter its upright and spreading growth habit. This will create a full specimen when mature. Prune mature plants after the fruit has set.

Potential Problems

Pests: Scale and mealybugs; spider mites in hot and dry conditions

Foliar disease: Not susceptible

Root disease: Highly susceptible, especially in cool, wet soils and low light conditions

olive

pineapple guava

banana

dwarf pomegranate

2. The Rest of the Tropical Fruit Basket

Acerola · Australian Beach Cherry
Avocado · Banana · Dragon Fruit
Dwarf Pomegranate · Fig · Guava
June Plum · Miracle Berry · Naranjilla
Noni · Olive · Orangeberry · Papaya
Passion Fruit · Peanut Butter Fruit
Pineapple · Pineapple Guava · Rose Apple
Sapodilla · Star Fruit · Tree Tomato

Acerola

Malpighia glabra

mal-PEE-gee-uh GLAY-bra

Acerola, also called Barbados cherry, has long been loved for its sweet-tasting berries and high vitamin C content. In South America it is well known for its health properties and is regularly added to fruit drinks, smoothies, and shakes. The acerola cherry has 30 times more vitamin C than citrus and is finally being recognized as a superfood. This little cherry packs a big punch for its size.

Acerola tolerates dry soil and air conditions, making it a great candidate for northern container culture. Under high light and warm temperatures, an abundance of cherrylike fruits appear. The flowers and fruit often form along the woody stems and small branches; fruit usually doesn't appear on new growth and dominant terminal branches at the top of the plant. Acerola plants grown in containers outdoors will set fruit better because of exposure to strong sun and temperatures above 80°F (27°C), along with the work of pollinating insects. Indoors in cooler temperatures, plants will often flower but fail to set fruit.

Plant Particulars

Size and form
3–4 feet with pruning; upright shrub

Bloom season
Year-round in its native habitat; in containers in the North, spring until fall

Fruiting season
Intermittently year-round in tropical and subtropical regions; primarily summer in the North (container-grown plants)

Family
Malpighiaceae

Origin
The Caribbean, Central America, and south Texas

Acerola

Growing Conditions

Light: Full sun; will grow and flower in partial sun with limited fruit set

Soil: Well-drained potting mix

Minimum indoor temperature: 60°F (15°C) to maintain active growth; can tolerate temperatures in the 40s and 50s (4° to 15°C) for short durations. In the South, can tolerate temperatures to just below freezing as long as daytime temperatures are warm.

Hardiness outdoors: Zone 10

Care

Fertilizing: Moderate levels of a balanced fertilizer. Excessive fertilizer and low light will cause soft rank growth and reduced flowering.

Pruning: For best fruiting, prune to encourage lateral woody branches and stems (see page 134). Plants maintained at a height of 3–5 feet will remain productive. Once plants reach desired height, the tallest growth can be trimmed back anytime growth is excessive.

Potential Problems

Pests: Aphids, especially in low light conditions or with excessive fertilizer

Foliar disease: Not susceptible

Root disease: Not susceptible; strong root system

ABOVE LEFT AND RIGHT: When grown in containers in the North, acerola blooms its pretty pink head off from spring through fall, but it produces cherries mainly during the summer.

Australian Beach Cherry

Eugenia reinwardtiana

yoo-JEE-nee-uh rine-war-dee-AY-nuh

Australian beach cherry is the perfect potted cherry. It's a marvelous container plant for gardeners with limited space and is perfect for windowsill culture. It tolerates dry soil and air as long as temperatures are above freezing. Australian beach cherry constantly produces shiny bright red cherries that are both delicious and beautiful. Their unique flavor is on the sweet side, and the fruits have a pulpy, fleshy inside, much like the texture of a peach.

This slow-grower begins fruiting as a young plant, often at only a foot tall. In its native habitat it flowers and fruits seasonally. When grown as a container plant under warm temperatures and bright light, however, it will fruit nearly year-round, stopping only for a few weeks in the darkest part of the year. Be sure to place in direct sun on a windowsill or in a sunroom or greenhouse. Once an Australian beach cherry reaches several feet in height, it becomes quite productive and bears in waves. The fruits turn quickly from green to red. Once the color has fully changed, harvest time is at hand. The plants will tolerate low light indoors during winter but will stop producing fruit. Once placed outside in full sun, vigorous growth and fruiting resume.

We propagate this cherry by seed. It takes a couple of years for seedlings to grow to 12 inches tall. It can also be propagated by air layering, and layered plants will produce fruit within a year (see Air Layering on page 141).

Plant Particulars

Size and form
2–4 feet with pruning; upright branching shrub

Bloom season
Year-round when grown at temperatures above 60°F (15°C) and in full to partial sun

Fruiting season
Year-round

Family
Myrtaceae

Origin
Tropical northeastern Australia

Australian beach cherry

Once they reach a foot in height, Australian beach cherry plants start producing cherries. Heavy fruit production begins when plants are 2–3 feet tall.

TOP RIGHT: Save the seeds from the ripe cherries and plant them to propagate your own plants.

Growing Conditions

Light: Full to partial sun

Soil: Well-drained potting mix

Minimum indoor temperature: 35°F (2°C)

Hardiness outdoors: Zone 10

Care

Fertilizing: Moderate levels of a balanced fertilizer; apply weekly or every other week when actively growing.

Pruning: Prune anytime growth is excessive to maintain size. Although flowers and fruit will be lost, the plant will flower again soon after pruning.

Potential Problems

Pests: Mealybugs if grown near infested plants

Foliar disease: Not susceptible except outdoors in south Florida

Root disease: Not susceptible; strong root system

⊙→ Not Quite a Cherry

Despite its name, the Australian beach cherry is not a relative of the sweet cherry and sour cherry that we grow in our backyards. Those cherries belong to the Rose family, while Australian beach cherry is a member of the Myrtle family. Native to the northeastern tropical areas of Australia, this shrub is often found growing on beachfronts there. It's also called Cedar Bay cherry, after a bay along the northeast Australian coast.

Avocado

Persea americana

PER-see-ah ah-mer-ih-KAY-nah

Avocados are well known as houseplants, but beware of the drawbacks of trying to start a plant from an avocado pit. Such plants hardly ever fruit, and if they do, the fruit quality is poor. Grafted clonal varieties are the best choice to produce fruit. When grown in a 14- to 16-inch container, a young grafted plant will begin to bear two to three years after planting.

Avocado trees are fast-growing bushy plants that can live outdoors after signs of frost are gone in the spring. Protect the trees from sunscald by keeping them out of direct sunlight for the first several days. Gradually move them into direct sun after that. Moving the trees to a cool spot indoors such as a conservatory, sunroom, or greenhouse for the winter helps set flower buds for the following spring.

Tasty avocados are low in calories and contain no cholesterol. Plus, eating them may help raise levels of high-density lipoproteins (HDLs), also known as "good cholesterol." The fruit's shiny lime-green skin turns dark green when ripe. Avocados will grow and ripen on the tree for at least three months; with 'Day' avocado trees, the fruit will ripen for six months.

You can pick avocados as soon as they reach mature size and allow ripening to continue on a tabletop or in the refrigerator. However, we like to leave our avocados on the plant as long as possible because of their ornamental appeal.

The varieties listed on page 57 have cold hardiness, which is a plus for avocado lovers. These varieties are self-pollinating, but we like to grow 'Day' and 'Brogdon' together just to be sure we will get good cross-pollination.

Plant Particulars

Size and form
3–6 feet with pruning; upright tree

Bloom season
March and April

Fruiting season
'Mexicolo': June and July; 'Brogdon': July to September; 'Day': August and September

Family
Lauraceae

Origin
The Caribbean and South and Central America

'Day' avocado

Recipes from the Tropical Kitchen

Guacamole "Gwawk"

Whenever we visit Barbara Glass (Laurelynn's mother) in Florida, she always serves an appetizer we call "Gwawk," her version of the classic guacamole recipe. This delicious quick recipe is one of our family's favorites. It's easy to make and nutritious.

2   chilled ripe avocados, peeled and
      pitted
3   garlic cloves, minced
      Juice from ½ lemon
      Sea salt
      Rice crackers

Mash together the avocados, garlic, and lemon juice. Add salt to taste. Serve on rice crackers.

Serves 4 to 6

'Mexicola' avacados have a thin rind and a delicious buttery flavor.

Growing Conditions

Light: Full sun year-round

Soil: Well-drained peat-based potting mix

Minimum indoor temperature: 35°F (2°C)

Hardiness outdoors: Zone 8b; can withstand temperatures as cold as 18°F (−8°C) for short durations

Care

Fertilizing: Moderate feeder. Use a balanced fertilizer; stop in late summer so the wood hardens off. Overfertilized plants form fewer new buds.

Pruning: Prune right after fruit set to maintain height and form. To avoid cutting off next year's flower buds, prune no later than June.

Potential Problems

Pests: Not susceptible

Foliar disease: Little susceptibility when grown in containers in the North; outside in the South, plants may suffer from scab (brown patches on the leaves) and powdery mildew (a white powdery coating on leaves). Use sulfur sprays to control scab; neem oil is effective for powdery mildew. (See page 146 for more information on neem.)

Root disease: Susceptible; results in stunting of plants

'Day' is by far the easiest avocado variety to fruit in a pot as a small plant. The medium-sized fruit has a tapered neck and is very easy to peel.

'Brogdon' has black skin like a 'Hass' avocado and is a good cross-pollinator.

'Mexicola' has a dense growth habit, small leaves, and small fruit.

Banana

Musa species

MEW-suh

Growing your own bananas in a pot is always a conversation starter, but harvesting the small bananas is even more impressive. With their tropical look, bananas will receive well-deserved attention in any space, whether grown in a pot inside, placed on an outdoor patio, or planted directly into a summer garden. Most banana plants need ample feed, plenty of water, and high levels of sunlight for quick, lush growth.

Horticulturally speaking, banana plants sprout from a bulb. Once a banana plant is mature, a flower stem travels up the inside of the trunk (technically known as a pseudostem) and emerges at the top. The flower head hangs down gracefully, and the first section of stem contains the female flowers that will become the bunch of bananas once they're pollinated. Male flowers then appear on the stem as the flower head continues to elongate. Bunches of bananas are called "hands." Once the fruits form, you can let the bunch hang on for several months until the bananas start to ripen to a golden yellow. Or pick the bananas when they're still green and allow them to ripen off the plant. After harvest, the flowering stem or pseudostem needs to be cut back to the ground. New offshoots, or pups, that have appeared during the growing season around the central stem will then replace the old plant. You can divide and pot up these pups if desired or leave them to grow in the same pot. Keep in mind, though, that bananas are fast-growing plants that can easily overwhelm their neighbors in a pot.

Many banana varieties grow too tall for most houses and home greenhouses; some of the best dwarf varieties for indoors are listed on page 59.

Size and form
3–6 feet; upright herbaceous plant

Bloom season
Intermittent throughout the year

Fruiting season
Year-round

Family
Musaceae

Origin
Tropical West Africa

Dwarf banana

Regulating Ripening

Commercial bananas that are harvested green are ripened by exposure to ethylene gas. However, bananas naturally emit ethylene gas. As the fruit ripens, sugar content increases and starch content goes down.

Let your green bananas ripen the old-fashioned way: leave them out at room temperature. Optimal temperatures are 68–70°F (20–21°C) with 90 percent humidity.

If timing is important, put your green bananas in a cool spot, about 58°F (14°C), to slow the ripening process. They will keep for up to 20 days.

ABOVE: 'Super Dwarf Cavendish' is also called apple banana because it bears such small bananas. It fruits when only 3–4 feet tall.

Growing Conditions

Light: Full sun

Soil: Well-drained potting mix

Minimum indoor temperature: Most cultivars, 60°F (15°C); 'Super Dwarf Cavendish' and 'Rajapuri' tolerate temperatures as low as 40°F (4°C), although growth slows or stops and plants may become dormant

Hardiness outdoors: Most cultivars, Zone 9; 'Rajapuri' can be grown outside in Zone 8 if mulched over winter

Care

Fertilizing: Heavy feeders; provide constant fertilizer, especially when temperatures are warm.

Pruning: Remove yellowing leaves as needed; cut back to soil level after harvest.

Potential Problems

Pests: Some susceptibility to spider mites in dry, warm conditions

Foliar disease: Susceptible to a fungus that results in brown patches and damaged leaves when temperatures fall below 60°F (15°C)

Root disease: Not highly susceptible, except in poorly drained soil

Lady finger banana (*Musa acuminata* 'Dwarf Lady Finger') is valued for its small, finger-sized bananas and slender growth. It produces deliciously sweet bananas within a year or two, flowering and fruiting when less than 4 feet tall.

Apple banana (*M. acuminata* 'Super Dwarf Cavendish') is a miniature "tree," a shorter form of 'Dwarf Cavendish' that grows only 3–4 feet tall. It will form a hand (bunch) of bananas within two to three years. If you remove all but a few side pups, however, the rate of fruit production will increase. Sometimes this variety forms its hand of bananas inside the flower stem. This is called "choking." If this happens, make a lateral cut in the pseudostem and pull the bananas out. Be sure to do this early in the flowering/fruiting cycle.

'Rajapuri' (*M. balbisiana* 'Rajapuri') bears when it reaches 6 feet tall. This will take 12 to 18 months.

'Vente Cohol' (*M. balbisiana* 'Vente Cohol') is the earliest fruiting banana; it can produce mature hands of bananas within a year. Plants eventually reach 5 feet tall.

A banana flower is both beautiful to look at and delicious to eat.

Using All Parts of the Plant

Leaves. Wrap foods in banana leaves to seal in moisture and nutrients. Good candidates include codfish with herbs, or a favorite Thai dish of sticky rice and coconut milk porridge (*khao dome*). A small pork roast or beef roast can be slow-cooked in banana leaves for delicious flavor.

Pseudostems. The hearts (insides of the banana stems) are eaten as a vegetable in Southeast Asia. They are rinsed several times in salt water, chopped, and then cooked in lime juice and coconut milk for flavor.

Flowers. In Southeast Asia, the banana flower is considered a delicacy and is often chopped up and stir-fried with spices. For a special touch, use the magenta-colored banana flower as a serving dish. The flower is said to be an effective cure for painful menstrual disorders and is also considered good for lactating mothers; it is high in vitamins A and C.

Green bananas. Unripe bananas can be sliced and fried in oil, then served as chips.

Ripe bananas. A great source of vitamin B_6 and potassium. Slice them onto cereal or eat them straight up. Ripe bananas make a delicious purée for cooking.

'Dwarf Lady Finger' banana

Preparing Banana Leaves

Here's how to prepare banana leaves for use in cooking.

1. Harvest fresh banana leaves.

2. Clean the leaves with water and dry thoroughly.

3. With scissors, cut away yellow or brown damage. Make sure the leaves aren't split.

4. Cut the leaves into 8½-by-11-inch pieces.

If you have extras that you don't need right away, stack them one atop the other, with plastic wrap separating each layer, and freeze. When you want to use some frozen leaves, remove as many as you need from the packaging, and return the rest to your freezer. Then thaw the leaves you selected for about two hours at room temperature. Rinse the partially thawed leaves in cold water to soften them and to remove any debris. Wipe the leaves with a cloth on both sides to remove excess water.

Dragon Fruit

Hylocereus undatus

hy-loh-KER-ee-us un-DAY-tus

Plant Particulars

Size and form
4–6 feet with support; orchid cactus with sprawling vines

Bloom season
Summer

Fruiting season
Late summer and fall

Family
Cactaceae

Origin
Tropical Americas

Dragon fruit is grown not only for its spectacular large red fruits but also for its fragrant nighttime blossoms. Although each blossom lasts only one night, new blooms appear repeatedly all summer long. (This plant also goes by the name night-blooming cereus.) It can take several years for a rooted cutting to reach its fruiting stage (4–5 feet), but then it will produce three or four crops per year.

Dragon fruit is easy to grow. It is an orchid cactus, a member of the large epiphytic or tree-dwelling group within the Cactus family. Epiphytes are plants that do not need to grow with roots in soil; they are also known as air plants. When grown in containers in well-drained potting mix, the plants will form roots.

Dragon fruit's unique top growth is made up of three-sided segments, which vigorously extend outward and upward. These heavy vines need lots of support. A 16- to 18-inch container with a sturdy pot trellis will hold this sprawling plant for years.

Once flowering has begun, you will need to hand-pollinate (see page 134). Do this in the evening once the flower is fully open. From the base of the flower, a round-to-oblong fruit forms. Prominent scales on the outside rind of this baseball-sized fruit give dragon fruit its name. Within a month or two, the fruit will turn red and be ready to pick. The interior texture is a cross between a pear and a kiwi; the taste is sweet, soft, and quite delicious. Plus, dragon fruits are high in antioxidants. The interior of the fruit is white, but there are hybrid varieties with a red or purple interior.

Dragon fruit

Beneath the exotic scaly green-and-red rind of the dragon fruit is succulent white flesh flecked with small black seeds (top right).

How to Slay (Eat) a Dragon Fruit

Angel, our 11-year-old daughter, says her favorite fruit in this book is dragon fruit. "Don't worry about the scales," she advises. "They're just fun to look at, but the fruit is sweet and yummy."

Angel offers two choices of how to eat a dragon fruit:

A. Cut the red, scaled fruit in half and scoop out the flesh like a soft-boiled egg.

B. Slice into quarters and peel back the skin until the flesh pops out.

Growing Conditions

Light: Full to partial sun; the more light the better

Soil: Well-drained potting mix

Minimum indoor temperature: 50°F (10°C); can withstand temperatures down to freezing for short periods as long as the soil is dry

Hardiness outdoors: Zone 10

Care

Fertilizing: Moderate feeders; fertilize weekly or every other week with a dilute balanced fertilizer when temperatures are warm; discontinue in fall and winter. Restrict watering in winter too, especially in the North. In the first years of growth, water and fertilizer can be continued during winter to accelerate growth and maturity if plants are kept warm.

Pruning: Prune in the late summer and fall after flowering to maintain size.

Potential Problems

Pests: Mealybugs can be a minor problem

Foliar disease: Susceptible under cool temperatures and high humidity

Root disease: Susceptible in cold, wet soil

Dwarf Pomegranate

Punica granatum 'Nana'

PU-nih-kuh grah-NAH-tum

Plant Particulars

Size and form
1–3 feet; bushy shrub or tree

Bloom season
Spring into summer

Fruiting season
Summer and fall

Family
Punicaceae

Origin
Iran to the Himalayas

Pomegranate juice is a popular beverage because of its antioxidant content, and restaurants and martini bars have joined the health craze by offering pomegranate martinis as an indulgent drink that's good for you too. Whether you drink martinis or not, you'll love growing a dwarf pomegranate plant for its bright showy blooms that smother the plant in color all summer. Delicious fruits quickly follow.

This small shrub is perfect for a large windowsill. Its funnel-shaped reddish orange flowers especially stand out when the plant is cultured as a bonsai. The 1- to 2-inch fruits ripen from green to red. As your pomegranate plant ages and grows bigger, you'll reap a bigger harvest because larger plants have more energy to hold the fruit while it ripens. The fruit is tart, although sweeter when sun-ripened on the tree.

Dwarf pomegranate tolerates dry soil and air, but you should avoid letting your plant dry to the point of a severe wilt. Most pomegranates are deciduous and need winter dormancy with a chilling period of temperatures between 35 and 55°F (2° and 13°C) to promote bud formation. 'Nana', however, seems to be exempt from a chilling requirement; that, along with its smaller size, makes it the best choice for indoor culture.

Dwarf pomegranate

TOP LEFT AND RIGHT: Showy red-dish orange blooms smother a dwarf pomegranate plant all summer long.

BOTTOM LEFT AND RIGHT: Each plant bears four to six fruit per crop. To eat the fruit, split it in half and pop out the juicy (but sour) seeds for eating.

Growing Conditions

Light: Full to partial sun

Soil: Well-drained potting mix

Minimum indoor temperature: 35°F (2°C)

Hardiness outdoors: Zone 8

Care

Fertilizing: Moderate feeder; supply a balanced fertilizer weekly or every other week. Reduce or stop in winter.

Pruning: Prune after flowering is complete.

Potential Problems

Pests: Aphids on soft new growth; mealybugs and whiteflies

Foliar disease: Few problems

Root disease: Generally not susceptible, but when young plants are grown under high fertility and heat stress, root and stem disease can cause sudden wilt

Fig

Ficus carica

FYE-kus KAIR-ih-kuh

To grow figs successfully in pots in the North, plants need an early start in the spring and then a place that remains warm in the fall to ensure that fruit will ripen. Outdoors, choose a warm, bright spot where trees will be protected from late frosts, such as by a south-facing wall. If growing conditions are kept warm in the wintertime, figs will hold their foliage year-round. Plants go dormant and drop their leaves if exposed to cold temperatures, lower light, or short daylength. If you don't have room to bring your fig trees inside your house for the winter, try keeping them in your garage or basement, as long as temperatures don't drop too much below freezing.

'Petite Negra' produces medium-sized plump, juicy blackish purple figs. It's perfect for the indoor or patio gardener since it starts fruiting when less than 12 inches tall. 'Petite Negra' is ornamental as well, with its mitten-shaped green leaves and ripening plump fruit. Grow in full sun on a table by the window or outside in warm temperatures.

'Chicago Hardy' can be grown in containers or planted directly into the ground in the North if mulched. (See Overwintering Figs in the North on page 69.) It can take subfreezing temperatures better than most, dying back in the fall and resprouting in the spring. Its medium-sized fruits ripen in late summer to early fall. This easy-to-grow fig, also known as 'Bensonhurst Purple', originated in Sicily.

'Black Mission' has the ability to produce two sizeable crops a season. The outstanding sweetness of its fruit, whether eaten fresh or dried, is why 'Black Mission' has become the most famous fig in cultivation. Though less tolerant of cold than 'Chicago Hardy', it can be wintered outside in the North if mulched and wrapped. Or position it indoors by a sunny window and watch it grow year-round.

Plant Particulars

Size and form
3–5 feet; bush or small tree

Bloom season
Spring through summer

Fruiting season
Summer into fall

Family
Moraceae

Origin
The Mediterranean and Southwest Asia

Fig

'Petite Negra' fig trees produce an abundance of fruit.

RIGHT: A split fig shows off its sweet, seeded amber pulp.

Growing Conditions

Light: Full sun

Soil: Adaptable to most potting mixes

Minimum indoor temperature: 25°F (−4°C)

Hardiness outdoors: 'Petite Negra', Zone 8; 'Chicago Hardy', Zone 6; 'Black Mission', Zone 7. In Zones 6 and 7, trees need winter protection with mulch outdoors. No winter protection is needed in Zone 8 and warmer.

Care

Fertilizing: Moderate feeder; feed weekly or every other week with a balanced fertilizer during active growth. Reduce or stop during winter.

Pruning: Prune in late winter to early spring before growth resumes to maintain a shapely specimen.

Potential Problems

Pests: Not susceptible except under dry conditions, and then beware of spider mites

Foliar disease: Not susceptible

Root disease: Not susceptible; strong root system

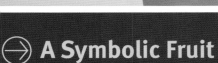

⊙→ A Symbolic Fruit

The fig tree has long been a symbol of abundance, fertility, and sweetness, going back to biblical times. In Mediterranean custom, figs represent strong family ties, memories, and loyalties; a family gathering is never complete without fresh figs or a fig dish.

Popular for its outstanding sweetness, 'Black Mission' will easily produce two sizeable crops of figs every year.

Facts About Figs

- According to USDA data, dried 'Black Mission' figs are one of the richest plant sources of dietary fiber, copper, manganese, magnesium, potassium, calcium, and vitamin K.

- Figs have a laxative effect and contain many antioxidants such as flavonoids and polyphenols.

- Eating two medium-sized figs per day has been reported to produce a significant increase in plasma antioxidant capacity.

- Figs can produce two crops per year. The spring fruit, called the breba crop, is borne on the previous season's growth. The main crop forms on the current season's growth and ripens in the fall.

- Figs must ripen on the tree. Once they are picked they do not ripen.

- Fresh figs last only two to three days in the refrigerator. However, you can enjoy your figs for six to eight months simply by drying them in the sun for four or five days or in a dehydrator for 10–12 hours.

Recipes from the Tropical Kitchen

Balsamic Fig Reduction

This fig reduction can be used in sauces, appetizers, desserts, and more. If you use a premium-quality balsamic vinegar, it can be expensive to make, but a little goes a long way.

- ½ cup fresh 'Black Mission' fig pulp
- ½ cup balsamic vinegar
- ½ cup confectioners' sugar, plus more as needed
- 1 teaspoon vanilla

Combine the fresh fig pulp and balsamic vinegar in a small saucepan. Simmer, stirring constantly, for about 30 minutes, until reduced to about 1½ cups. Add the confectioners' sugar, and cool. Sweeten to taste with more confectioners' sugar, if desired.

Use immediately or store in an airtight container in the refrigerator.

Makes about 1½ cups

'Chicago Hardy' tastes and looks a lot like 'Black Mission' fig, but 'Chicago Hardy' is much better at surviving cold northern winters.

 # Overwintering Figs in the North

This technique for protecting figs was passed on to us by Stanley Parchaiski of Waterford, Connecticut, and will work in areas as cold as Zone 5. Immigrant Italian gardeners have used a similar method for protecting figs in southern New England for decades.

In the fall, once the frost has killed the foliage, cut back your fig plant to 4–6 feet. If your plant is growing in a plastic container, sink the container in a garden bed so the soil in the pot is at ground level. (This method may not work as well for fig trees planted in terra-cotta or wooden containers.) If possible choose a spot against a south-facing wall, which will add more warmth and give protection in the spring when the plant first resumes growth.

Wrap heavy string or rope around the stems and branches and pull them together to form an upright column, which will look rather like a long bundle of kindling. Bind the bundle as tightly as possible without damaging the plant. Don't be afraid of breaking the tree's main stem; it has tremendous flexibility.

Wrap the bound column in pink fiberglass insulation. Use the roll type with the paper backing facing outward. Wrap from the ground up, and tie the insulation in place with string. Next, cover the entire column of insulation with a plastic tarp or plastic sheeting; tie that in place with string as well. For the final step, set a pot over the top like a hat to shed water. Mulch the base with some straw to insulate the roots.

Unwrap your tree the following spring, just after the danger of frost is past in your area. The plant will immediately leaf out and go into fruit; in fact, fruit may form even before the new leaves expand.

Guava

Psidium species

SIGH-dee-um

Plant Particulars

Size and form
3–6 feet; bushy evergreen shrub

Bloom season
Spring through summer

Fruiting season
Summer into fall

Family
Myrtaceae

Origin
Tropical Americas

Guavas are well known in the world of tropical fruits and are often marketed as superfruits for their antioxidant properties and high vitamin C content. Common guava, also called apple guava *(Psidium guajava),* has four times more vitamin C than a single orange.

Guava plants are grown either from seed or by cuttings and are fast growers if given good light and some fertilizer. Cutting-grown plants will flower sooner and make a generally smaller specimen. If grown from seed, it can take several years to bring a plant into fruit.

To grow as many guava fruits as possible on one shrub, you'll need to give the plant a lot of sunshine. Once fruiting size has been reached, flowers form on the new growth at the leaf axils.

During the winter if plants are situated in cool conditions where night-time temperatures drop below 60°F (15°C), pay special attention to avoid overwatering or overfertilizing to prevent root rot. Growing guavas in unglazed clay or terra-cotta pots will help maintain healthy roots.

In the South, pick guava fruits before they get too soft to avoid fruit fly problems. The fruits can be eaten firm or just on the point of turning soft.

'Nana', known as dwarf guava, is a variety we found in Maui. Right away we loved this smaller version of the commercial variety because it fits well on a large windowsill. Mature plants grow up to 3 feet tall and are easy to maintain at that size with pruning. The fruit, which can grow as long as 2 inches, has a powerfully packed interior. The flesh is pink, firm, sweet, and seeded.

'Purpurea' is a larger variety that has both ornamental and edible appeal. The fruit can grow to the size of a tennis ball. The flowers are pink rather than white and the fruit has purple mottling on the outside.

'Nana' guava

Clusters of lemon guava fruit are eaten skin and all. Their fleshy centers are soft and sweet when ripe.

BOTTOM LEFT: This mesmerizing strawberry guava flower resembles miniature fireworks.

BOTTOM RIGHT: Guava flowers burst forth with luminous pink petals, but 'Purpurea' guava then produces a purple-tinged fruit.

Growing Conditions

Light: Full sun; strawberry and lemon guava can tolerate partial sun

Soil: Well-drained potting mix

Minimum indoor temperature: 'Nana' and 'Purpurea', 40°F (4°C); strawberry and lemon guava, 32°F (0°C), but warmer temperatures promote faster growth

Hardiness outdoors: 'Nana' and 'Purpurea', Zone 10; strawberry and lemon guava, Zone 9

Care

Fertilizing: Apply a balanced fertilizer monthly during the active growing season; reduce or stop in the winter.

Pruning: Prune 'Nana' and 'Purpurea' before active growth begins in late winter, or prune selectively anytime growth is excessive. Flowers form on new growth; prune tip growth lightly after flowers appear to maintain plant size and form. Prune strawberry and lemon guava anytime growth is excessive; once fruit has ripened, moderate pruning does not interfere with future fruit development, because flowers will form on the older woody stem as well as young branches.

Potential Problems

Pests: Mealybugs; occasionally spider mites and aphids. In tropical areas, fruit flies have become a major guava pest. Strawberry and lemon guava may also suffer from scale.

Foliar disease: 'Nana' and 'Purpurea' are susceptible under highly humid conditions.

Root disease: 'Nana' and 'Purpurea' are susceptible when soil is cool and highly fertile. Reduce or eliminate fertilizer in the winter; allow potting mix to dry between waterings.

Strawberry guava (*Psidium littorale* var. *cattleianum*) is an exceptional potted fruit plant for the home, adapting well to low humidity and drought stress. Its attractive, shiny, deep green leaves and dense spreading habit make for a full, bushy plant that can also be grown as a standard. Strawberry guava boasts ¾- to 1-inch red to dark red fruits with a sweet, tangy flavor.

Lemon guava (*Psidium littorale* subsp. *littorale*) is closely related to strawberry guava but is less commonly grown. Its fruit is slightly larger and has a cleaner flavor with an overall sweet bouquet. Both lemon and strawberry guava are usually untroubled by disease problems.

June Plum

Spondias dulcis

SPON-dee-as DUL-sis

The June plum, also called ambarella, is a highly productive tropical tree that produces an abundance of oval golden fruit. We like the dwarf form, which often flowers and fruits within a year or two from seed. Flowers appear at the growing tips during active summer growth, and clusters of fruit follow. Winter brings a deciduous dormancy, with unripe green fruit hanging on the leafless branches for six to eight months. This unusual sight — a bare stem laden with fruit — looks like a carefully constructed holiday decoration. When spring arrives, it seems almost miraculous when new growth emerges, flowers appear, and the previous summer's fruit begins to ripen. When the fruit turns golden yellow, it can be picked and allowed to ripen to a slightly soft state. Peel the June plum and eat the pulp around the large fibrous seed. The sweet and slightly sour taste is well loved in its native Southeast Asia. The large fibrous seed inside can be planted to start another plant if so desired; plants can also be started from cuttings.

Plant Particulars

Size and growth
4–6 feet if pruned; upright deciduous tree

Bloom season
Summer

Fruiting season
Summer

Family
Anacardiaceae

Origin
Southeast Asia

June plum

These June plums are still unripe.

TOP RIGHT: As the fruits ripen, droplets of plant exudate (sugars) form on the skin.

Growing Conditions

Light: Full to partial sun

Soil: Well-drained potting mix

Minimum indoor temperature: 40°F (4°C)

Hardiness outdoors: Zone 10

Care

Fertilizing: Moderate feeder; fertilize regularly starting when new growth appears in the spring. Stop in winter once the leaves have dropped.

Pruning: Prune to maintain size after leaves have dropped in winter or after fruit has fallen in late summer.

Potential Problems

Pests: Few problems, although occasionally aphids appear on soft growth

Foliar disease: Few problems

Root disease: Not susceptible; strong root system

Miracle Berry

Synsepalum dulcificum

sin-SEP-ah-lum dul-SIF-ih-kum

The "miracle" is in this plant's gumdrop-sized red berry. When you eat the berry, it tricks your taste buds so that everything eaten after the berry tastes sweet, even sour lemons or limes. Be forewarned, though: eating too much sour fruit, even if it tastes sweet at the time, may leave your belly feeling somewhat sour afterward.

An upright growth habit and unusual prominently veined foliage make miracle berry, also called miracle fruit, an attractive container plant. Although a slow grower, once this plant reaches 1–2 feet, it produces abundantly. If kept in full sun and fertilized monthly, it fruits heavily twice a year. Plants that receive partial sun will produce fruit but will not be as productive. Miracle berry is self-pollinating. Outdoors, the wind and birds facilitate pollination; indoors, be sure to brush or shake the branches to ensure successful pollination.

We've been growing this plant for several years. After much experimentation, we discovered that the key to success is having the right soil pH: an acidic soil mixture is a must. Severe interveinal yellowing indicates an iron deficiency, a likely signal that the pH is out of balance. Edge burn can also be a problem with miracle berry. This can result from using chlorinated water or, more likely, from applying too much fertilizer.

Plant Particulars

Size and form
To 5 feet; upright tree

Bloom season
Intermittently year-round

Fruiting season
Intermittently year-round; heaviest in spring and fall

Family
Sapotaceae

Origin
Tropical West Africa

Miracle berry

Miracle berries ripen from green to red within a week and then hold on the plant for up to 2 months.

Growing Conditions

Light: Full to partial sun

Soil: An acidic soil mixture of half sphagnum peat moss and half perlite

Minimum indoor temperature: 60°F (15°C); can withstand lower temperatures for short periods

Hardiness outdoors: Zone 10

Care

Fertilizing: Moderate amounts of fertilizer once a month; sensitive to high salt levels, so use a very dilute fertilizer solution (¼ to ⅛ of label strength) to help prevent edge burn. Never feed when the soil is dry. If you see severe edge burn, leach the potting mix by flushing it with clear water. The brown-edged leaves will not turn green again, but new green leaves will appear.

Pruning: Slow-growing; needs only occasional pruning to maintain size. Prune after a heavy fruiting period or anytime growth is excessive.

Potential Problems

Pests: Not susceptible

Foliar disease: Not susceptible

Root disease: Not susceptible

 ## Sour Tastes Sweet

When it comes to figuring out how sour becomes sweet, we think it's nothing short of a miracle. But our 13-year-old son, Elijah (the math and science guy in the family), knows that the presence of an unstable compound in miracle berries changes the chemical properties in your mouth, which in turn changes the way your taste buds perceive flavors. Regardless of the mechanism, Elijah has tricked many friends and won many bets that a lemon will taste sweet if you eat the berry first. Here's how to turn heads and empty wallets:

1. Pluck one red miracle berry from your tree.

2. Put the whole berry in your mouth.

3. Do not bite into the berry (there is a seed inside). Instead, using your teeth, carefully work the skin and pulp off the seed.

4. Spit out the seed. If you like, you can save it for planting.

5. Don't swallow the pulp yet! Coat your entire mouth with the berry pulp, including the roof of your mouth and your tongue, before swallowing.

6. Savor the sweetness for 3 to 4 minutes, then bite into a sour lemon or a sour pickle. It will taste sweet too!

The effect on your taste buds will last from 20 minutes up to a few hours. After sampling a miracle berry in the afternoon, one of our customers went to a dinner party and drank an expensive dry red wine. This customer was puzzled by the oddly sweet flavor of what was supposed to be a spectacular dry wine. She wondered why the other guests were oohing and aahing — until she remembered the miracle berry!

Naranjilla

Solanum quitoense

soh-LAN-um kee-toh-EN-see

The naranjilla is a spectacular ornamental plant with hairy, heart-shaped purple leaves. It produces small, round orange fruits that can be eaten or juiced. One variety should be called ninja instead of naranjilla because of its formidable spikes, which protrude from both sides of the leaves; one of its common names is bed of nails. However, there is a spineless variety, which is less intimidating and easier to manage. Both varieties produce fruits a little larger than the size of a cherry tomato.

Naranjilla plants are perennials that will grow and fruit for years, but since they are rapid growers, they can be raised as annuals in the North, much like tomatoes. If you want to increase your supply of plants, save seed and sow it early in the season. Move young plants outside when the danger of frost is over. Plant them directly into the ground or grow them in containers. If given a long enough season, they will flower and produce fruit.

Naranjilla fruits start out green and are covered with fine hairs. When ripe, they turn orange and the hair is easily rubbed off. Usually, the fruit is squeezed to extract the acidic yet flavorful juice; sugar can be added to taste. You can also eat this fruit out of hand by scooping out the interior pulp and seeds; discard the outer skin.

Size and form
2–4 feet with pruning; upright herbaceous plant

Bloom season
Spring to fall in the North; year-round in the South

Fruiting season
Summer into fall

Family
Solanaceae

Origin
South America

Naranjilla

TOP LEFT AND RIGHT: Deep orange color means that these naranjilla fruits are ripe and ready to eat (rub off the fuzz first).

Naranjilla flowers keep producing an abundance of new fruit even while the green fruit is ripening.

Growing Conditions

Light: Full sun to partial shade

Soil: Well-drained potting mix

Minimum indoor temperature: 60°F (15°C); will tolerate temperatures down to freezing for short periods

Hardiness outdoors: Zone 10

Care

Fertilizing: Heavy feeders under warm growing conditions; apply balanced fertilizer once a week. Discontinue if temperatures are cool or light levels are low.

Pruning: Prune anytime growth is excessive.

Potential Problems

Pests: Susceptible to whiteflies, aphids, and spider mites

Foliar disease: Few problems

Root disease: Not susceptible in containers

Noni

Morinda citrifolia

mo-RIN-dah sih-trih-FOH-lee-uh

This tree flourishes in the lush tropical islands of French Polynesia. Also called Indian mulberry, in Southeast Asia it goes by the common name nhau. Noni is reported to be helpful in treating everything from colds, pain, and high blood pressure to cancer, diabetes, asthma, skin infections, depression, atherosclerosis, and arthritis. No wonder some have nicknamed the noni fruit "the fruit of the gods." Noni juice has become popular for its health benefits and is often marketed as Tahitian noni juice — but the noni you grow will be every bit as good as the "Tahitian" brand.

In its native habitat, noni reaches 15–20 feet tall and is considered one of the most beautiful and beneficial trees. In containers, noni will begin fruiting when it reaches 1–2 feet tall or once lateral branching has started. Given adequate light and warm temperatures, fruiting will continue nonstop.

The plant has shiny green elliptical leaves and a dense, full growth habit. The mature fruit is the size of a small potato. When ripe, it turns from green to yellow and white and has a pungent, offensive odor. In both Polynesia and Southeast Asia, noni has been eaten as a staple food, but only during periods of famine.

Plant Particulars

Size and form
4–8 feet with pruning; upright tree

Bloom season
Year-round

Fruiting season
Year-round

Family
Rubiaceae

Origin
Southeast Asia

Noni

It's a good thing that noni fruit promotes good health, because its blue cheese flavor and offensive odor would not win it any culinary awards.

Growing Conditions

Light: Full to partial sun

Soil: Well-drained potting mix

Minimum indoor temperature: 60°F (15°C); will not tolerate cold soils in containers for long periods

Hardiness outdoors: Zone 10

Care

Fertilizing: Moderate feeder; benefits from applications of a balanced fertilizer every other week as long as temperatures are warm.

Pruning: Prune to maintain size, but keep in mind that pruning new growth will reduce or delay fruiting.

Potential Problems

Pests: Some susceptibility to spider mites and aphids

Foliar disease: Susceptible under high humidity

Root disease: Susceptible in containers when soil is cool and wet

Gently Moving the Giants

Transferring a demure 2-foot lemon plant in an 8-inch pot from your deck to your living room is easy to do, but how about moving that 6-foot-tall noni or papaya tree in the 16-inch planter? Try these tips when you're faced with the task of moving large container plants.

- Plan ahead to stop watering, so you can move your plant when the soil is dry. Wet soil is heavy.
- Consider the space you are moving your plant into. Will the plant fit, or will you need to prune it to reduce the size? If you are planning to prune, make your cuts before you move the plant.

- Invest in a hand truck or a plant caddy. A plant caddy is simply a large round saucer mounted on wheels. We recommend wheel locks. Plant caddies make the job of moving plants much easier, whether you're transferring them from outdoors in, changing their indoor arrangement, or getting them out of the way on cleaning day.

Olive

Olea europaea

ˈOH-lee-ah yur-oh-PAY-ah

These fabulous, easy-to-grow plants have a rugged nature. They can withstand tremendous dryness in the soil and air. Plus they grow well under varied light levels. They also tolerate wide swings in temperatures, from just below freezing up to the triple digits. Their small, hard leaves are designed for harsh conditions, and they have few pest problems. It's no wonder that olives are grown as container plants throughout the world.

The trick to getting olives to set fruit lies with light and nighttime temperature. Olives need lots of sun during the growing season and several months of nighttime temperatures between 30 and 45°F (−1 and 7°C) during the winter in order to set flower buds. Container specimens can be left outside until temperatures start dropping into the 20s (−7 to −2°C) at night. Move containers into a warmer growing area, one that drops to temperatures from just below freezing up to the high 40s (4–9°C) at night. Although some direct sunlight is needed at this time, light levels can be lower than during the flowering and growing periods.

After several months of cold nights, bring olive plants into a warmer spot with higher light. White flowers that have no fragrance will form on the mature growth and release copious amounts of pollen. The growing area around the plant may turn white with pollen.

We recommend growing two varieties for cross-pollination to ensure good fruit set.

Size and form
4–6 feet in containers

Bloom season
Late winter through early spring

Fruiting season
Late summer through fall

Family
Oleaceae

Origin
The Mediterranean, Asia, and Africa

Olive

Curing Olives

Everyday olives are not eaten straight from the tree; they are cured in brine first to remove bitterness and give them their well-known and well-loved flavor. Curing olives is a simple but lengthy process. It usually takes three to six weeks.

There are five simple steps to curing olives:

1. Make a vertical cut into each olive without damaging the pit. Put the olives in a pottery crock, bowl, or pan.
2. Mix ¼ cup salt in 1 quart of water to make a brine. Pour the brine over the olives, making sure all the olives are covered.
3. Cover the container loosely with cheesecloth.
4. Shake, turn, or stir the container of olives daily.
5. Change the brine mixture once a week until the curing process has finished.

After three weeks, taste-test an olive to see if its bitterness has gone away. Continue tasting every five or six days until the taste seems right to you — then your olives are cured.

To store your home-cured olives, strain off the brine and put the olives in a glass jar. Make a new batch of brine, using the same proportions of salt and water. Combine 2 parts brine with 1 part red wine vinegar, and add enough of this mixture to cover the olives. Top off the jar with a layer of olive oil, usually about 1 tablespoon. If stored properly in a cool, dark place or in the refrigerator, cured olives will keep for up to one year.

Growing Conditions

Light: Full sun

Soil: Adaptable to most potting mixes

Minimum indoor temperature: 30°F (−1°C)

Hardiness outdoors: Zone 8

Care

Fertilizing: Moderate feeders; use a balanced fertilizer weekly or every other week during the active growing season; as summer changes to fall, discontinue to allow plants to harden off.

Pruning: After flowering, prune branches that are too long or gangly to maintain form and desired height. Flower buds form on new growth.

Potential Problems

Pests: Scale

Foliar disease: Not susceptible

Root disease: Can be a problem when soil remains cold and wet

ABOVE: Although olives are self-fertile, growing two varieties will improve fruit set. 'Arbequina' (left) and 'Manzanillo' (right) make great pollination companions.

'Arbequina' flowers at an early age, often when only 1 foot tall, and produces an abundance of tasty small dark olives. This olive from northern Spain is used both as a table olive and for its oil.

'Manzanillo', another Spanish olive, is one of the most widely grown varieties for its oil and its table appeal. 'Manzanillo' easily produces olives as soon as it reaches 3 feet tall.

Orangeberry

Glycosmis pentaphylla or *Limonia pentaphylla*

glye-KOS-mis pen-tuh-FIL-uh; li-MOH-nee-ah pen-tuh-FIL-uh

*N*orthern Australia has had a well-kept secret — until now. That secret is orangeberry, a delicious sweet fruit that has all the vitamin C of citrus packaged in a tiny berry. White flowers emerge on the flower heads over a period of several weeks, and flowering can continue for months. Small green berries form that eventually ripen to orange. The shiny berries are somewhat translucent, showing the single seed inside each. Ripe berries have a resinous aftertaste reminiscent of gin, which is why they're also known as gin berries. However, the only intoxication you'll get from gin berry is the joy of seeing a full bushy specimen loaded with berries waiting to be plucked.

Give these productive plants sunshine and warmth and they will flower and fruit continuously. They are generally grown from seed or cuttings. Cutting-grown plants will begin flowering and fruiting immediately once rooted, so they are the best choice for small-space gardeners. Seed-grown plants start flowering and fruiting when they reach 1–2 feet and will eventually grow to be larger specimens overall.

Plant Particulars

Size and form
3–6 feet with pruning; small tree

Bloom season
Year-round in its native range; spring through fall as a container plant in the North

Fruiting season
Year-round

Family
Rutaceae

Origin
Southeast Asia and northern Australia

Orangeberry

Given plenty of sunshine and warmth, a cutting-grown orangeberry plant will flower and fruit year-round, beginning soon after planting.

Growing Conditions

Light: Prefers full sun, although it will grow and flower in partial sun

Soil: Well-drained potting mix

Minimum indoor temperature: If year-round flowering and fruiting is desired, grow at 60°F (15°C); will tolerate temperatures down to freezing

Hardiness outdoors: Zone 10

Care

Fertilizing: Moderate feeder; apply a balanced fertilizer every other week when temperatures are warm and light is adequate. Slow or stop during winter.

Pruning: Sometimes necessary to maintain form and height; mature plants tend to get tall and lanky. Prune after a heavy fruiting cycle, or in winter before active growth resumes. Plants quickly resprout and flower after hard pruning.

Potential Problems

Pests: Aphids on soft new growth

Foliar disease: Not susceptible

Root disease: Not susceptible; strong, vigorous root system

Papaya

Carica papaya

KAIR-ih-kuh puh-PIE-yuh

Papaya is exotic and deliciously edible. Papayas in general have a sweet flavor, something like a cross between a mild-flavored cantaloupe and a watermelon. The texture of the flesh is more like a cantaloupe.

Standard commercial seed-grown papayas can grow up to 12 feet tall but they begin fruiting at around 4 feet tall. Plant height is determined largely by genetics, but the size of papaya fruits and leaf stem length are directly related to the size of the pot. Fruits can be huge; those of 'TR Hovey' can weigh as much as 4 pounds. When the fruit develops, the plant's growth slows down until the fruit ripens and is harvested; growth then resumes.

Papayas are very adaptable in terms of reproduction. When grown from seed, the plants can be dioecious (each plant bearing only male or female flowers) or monoecious (having both male and female flowers on the same plant). Some plants can even produce perfect flowers, which means that each blossom contains both male and female reproductive structures. During the winter months, they may lose their leaves if light level drops and temperatures drop below 65°F (18°C), but new leaves will appear in the spring.

'TR Hovey' papaya is a dwarf form of the commercial papaya that was hybridized for hydroponic culture and is perfect for growing in pots. 'TR Hovey' needs sunny, warm growing conditions and soil temperature of 60°F (15°C) or warmer. With the right cultural conditions, 'TR Hovey' will grow quickly and produce ripe fruit in as little as one year's time. Bring it inside for the winter and do not take outside until air temperatures are well above 60°F (15°C). If conditions are too cold, the plant can develop root disease and collapse. Fruit will start developing only 12 inches from the base of the plant. We have a plant that grew to 3 feet tall and set big fruits only 10 months after planting.

Plant Particulars

Size and form
'TR Hovey' 5 feet, babaco 3–4 feet; upright trees

Bloom season
Year-round

Fruiting season
Year-round depending upon temperature and light level

Family
Caricaceae

Origin
Ecuador, northwestern Andes, and New World tropics

'TR Hovey' papaya

Recipes from the Tropical Kitchen

Martha Stewart's Papaya Sorbet

A longtime fan of Logee's greenhouses, Martha Stewart has a very green thumb. She grows an impressive array of tropical plants, including several papaya plants. We brought Martha a 'TR Hovey' papaya when we visited her at her farm in Bedford, New York. She is a gracious hostess, warm and welcoming.

- ⅓ cup sugar
- 1 cup water
- 3 pounds fresh red-ripe papayas (about 1½ medium), peeled, halved, seeded, and chopped
- ½ cup fresh lime juice (3 to 4 limes total)
- 1 tablespoon honey
   Thin lime slices for garnish

In a medium saucepan, bring the sugar and water to a boil. Reduce the heat and simmer, stirring occasionally, until the sugar has dissolved and the mixture is syrupy, about 4 minutes. Let cool completely. Purée the papayas, lime juice, and honey in a food processor. Transfer to a medium bowl. Stir in the sugar syrup. Chill the mixture in an ice cream maker according to the manufacturer's instructions. Transfer to an airtight container and freeze for at least 2½ hours (up to 1 week). Serve garnished with lime slices.

Serves 4

'TR Hovey' papaya's ripe golden flesh has a sweet tropical-fruity flavor.

Growing Conditions

Light: Full sun

Soil: Well-drained potting mix

Minimum indoor temperature: Most productive when grown warm, above 60°F (15°C); babaco will tolerate lower temperatures, down to 32°F (0°C), for short periods

Hardiness outdoors: 'TR Hovey', Zone 10; babaco, Zone 9

Care

Fertilizing: Light to moderate feeders; fertilize once or twice a month until active growth stops, then reduce or stop in winter.

Pruning: Generally not needed. To reduce size, prune only after you harvest fruit, when plants are growing vigorously; don't cut back during cold weather.

Potential Problems

Pests: Two-spotted spider mites in dry, warm conditions

Foliar disease: Not susceptible

Root disease: Susceptible when soil stays overly moist and cool

Babaco (*Papaya × heilbornii* var. *pentagona)*, also called mountain papaya, has a more slender form, is more contained, and is slower growing than 'TR Hovey'. Babaco will produce fruit in a 6- to 8-inch pot. Each fruit hangs down from an individual stem; wait to harvest until the fruit turns a full golden color. The juicy, seedless fruit has a somewhat tart and distinctive flavor. When we first cut open this fruit, we were pleasantly surprised by its seedless nature; most papayas are packed full of little black seeds that need to be scraped from the flesh.

Passion Fruit

Passiflora species

pass-ih-FLOR-uh

Plant Particulars

Size and form
3–6 feet with support; woody vine

Bloom season
Throughout the year, depending on species and variety

Fruiting season
Spring through fall

Family
Passifloraceae

Origin
Tropical Americas

Passionflowers are well loved for their captivating flower structure, and certain varieties are also cherished for their sweet edible fruit. Passion fruit flavor is tart, light, and tangy. To produce fruit, most varieties need cross-pollination, either by different varieties in the same species or by other pollen-bearing species. In addition, hand-pollination is necessary for indoor plants; see page 134. Each passionflower is open for only one day, but flowers usually bloom in daily succession, providing many opportunities for hand-pollination.

To grow passion fruit plants, you'll need a love for vigorous, rambling vines. Use a stake, trellis, or hanging basket to support your passionflowers and give them a sunny exposure. However you decide to grow them, remember to occasionally pull back the reaching vines and redirect them to either the stakes, the trellis, or the main mass of vines. If enough growing space is available, you can let them ramble unrestricted; they'll extend many feet in length. The flowers form on the growing tips under high light and proper day length. One common problem is the aborting of young buds (bud blast), which is almost always caused by insufficient light or too much fertilizer.

Passiflora edulis, native to South America, is a good choice for beginning fruit growers because it is self-fertile and sets fruit easily. *P. edulis* 'McCain' bears yellow fruit; 'Possum Purple' is noted for its purple fruit. The fruit of both varieties has sweet pulp. 'McCain' is less vigorous but will flower and fruit as a small plant. 'Possum Purple' usually grows larger before it flowers. Even without hand-pollination, 'McCain' and 'Possum Purple' will easily form fruit, flowering from spring to fall. Harvest fruit when the color changes from green to yellow or purple, or when it falls from the vine.

'McCain' passion fruit

'Possum Purple' starts to produce its unusual purple fruit after only one season when it's given plenty of sun.

Growing Conditions

Light: Full sun

Soil: Well-drained potting mix

Minimum indoor temperature: 60°F (15°C); tolerates lower temperatures but susceptibility to root disease increases

Hardiness outdoors: Zone 10; protect from frost or plant against a foundation or wall

Care

Fertilizing: Moderate feeders; provide a balanced fertilizer weekly or every other week during the growing season. Excessive fertilizer can reduce flowering.

Pruning: Prune at the beginning of the active growing season or at least several months before the flowering season begins to maintain size. Exceptions: prune *P. miniata* 'Maui' in summer; prune *P. alata* 'Ruby Glow' and giant granadilla in late spring, once the flowering season has passed.

Potential Problems

Pests: Spider mites

Foliar disease: Few problems

Root disease: Susceptible in cool, wet conditions; *P. edulis* 'McCain' and *P. miniata* 'Maui' are the most susceptible

P. miniata 'Maui' bears round green-striped fruit that falls from the vine when ripe. This species is more challenging to grow in containers because of its susceptibility to root disease. Plus it requires high light levels during the winter. As a flowering vine, 'Maui' is unsurpassed in floral beauty and blooms abundantly from winter to spring. To prevent root disease issues, plants can be grafted onto *P. piresii* understock.

Giant granadilla *(P. quadrangularis)* and *P. alata* 'Ruby Glow' are similar in their growth, season of bloom, and fruiting. Both varieties have square stems and large, fragrant flowers. The vines need at least 6 to 12 months of growth before flowering begins. They bloom in either spring or fall, responding to the increase and decrease in day length. Fall is the most reliable blooming time for plants grown in the North. *P. quadrangularis* has the largest fruits of any passionflower; they can grow to the size of a small football. Fruit is ripe on both varieties when the color changes to a golden yellow.

Passionflower Pollination Needs

With the exception of *P. edulis* 'McCain' and 'Possum Purple', which can be self-fertile, passionflowers require hand-pollination by a different plant to produce fruit (see page 134). Here is a list of potential pollinators that bloom at the same time:

Fruiting Plant	Good Pollinators
P. miniata 'Maui'	use *P. caerulea*, *P.* 'Blue Bouquet', or another *P. miniata* variety
P. alata 'Ruby Glow'	use *P. caerulea*, *P. quadrangularis*, or another *P. alata* variety
P. edulis 'McCain' and 'Possum Purple'	(optional) use a flower from the same variety
P. quadrangularis	use *P. caerulea*, *P. alata*, or another *P. quadrangularis* variety

OPPOSITE: 'Maui' passionflower has captivating red flowers and attractive variegated fruit.

TOP: Although 'McCain' passion-flowers last only one day, its fruit can hold on the vine for months.

MIDDLE: 'Ruby Glow' sports one of the largest, most spectacular blossoms in the world of passionflowers, measuring 4 inches across.

BOTTOM: A great producer of large edible fruit, *Passiflora × decaisneana* is also grown for its large (4"), sweet-scented flowers that bloom in the spring and fall.

Peanut Butter Fruit

Bunchosia argentea

bun-CHO-see-ah ar-JEN-tee-uh

𝒩ame alone makes this novelty plant an interesting addition to any tropical fruit garden, and the fruit truly does have a hint of peanut butter flavor. Plants produce sprays of bright yellow blooms, which turn into 1-inch oval fruits that ripen to red. Fruits have a soft, sweet, dense pulp surrounding a large seed. In our experience, they are not heavy producers, usually producing only two fruits per flower stem.

Plants grown from cuttings or grafts flower the first year and go through several blooming cycles from March until October. The plants are naturally upright growers, and they can be maintained in 12- to 14-inch pots when mature. For good fruit set, they need warmth and sun. In the North, container-grown plants will yield fruit by the fall. If grown in a greenhouse or conservatory with abundant heat, fruiting will be earlier.

Plant Particulars

Size and form
4–6 feet with pruning; upright tree or shrub

Bloom season
Spring through fall

Fruiting season
Summer into fall

Family
Malpighiaceae

Origin
South America

Peanut butter fruit

About the size of a large olive, a peanut butter fruit is red outside, with sweet, sticky pulp that has a hint of peanut butter flavor inside.

RIGHT: Spires of soft yellow flowers are a lovely prelude to the captivating peanut butter fruit.

Growing Conditions

Light: Full sun to partial sun

Soil: Well-drained potting mix

Minimum indoor temperature: 40°F (4°C)

Hardiness outdoors: Zone 10

Care

Fertilizing: Moderate feeder; apply a balanced fertilizer throughout the growing season. Reduce or stop during winter.

Pruning: Prune at any time to maintain desired size; late winter before growth starts is best. Pruning during flowering will slow flower production, but pruned plants quickly begin to bloom and produce fruit again.

Potential Problems

Pests: Aphids and thrips; spider mites in dry, hot conditions

Foliar disease: Not susceptible

Root disease: Not susceptible; strong root system

 # Fun Facts about Peanut Butter Fruit

- It's easy to propagate by cuttings.
- It produces gorgeous blossoms.
- This plant likes it hot and sets more fruit in warm conditions.
- Ripening happens fast — in a matter of days, the fruit will turn red and become soft. Don't hold back on harvesting, or the fruit will drop off.

Pineapple

Ananus comosus

AH-nan-us kahm-OH-sus

Watching a pineapple plant grow and develop is quite entertaining. Spiky leaves fill the pot and a tiny pineapple forms, looking like it is precariously balanced on the crown of swordlike leaves. Flowers appear and open along the sides of the small fruit. After flowering is complete, the pineapple grows to full size and ripens to a golden color, and then the delicious harvest takes place. Simply cut the pineapple from the crown.

It takes about two years for a young plant to start producing fruit. During the growing period, be sure to give your pineapple plants lots of heat and direct sunlight and a bit of dryness between waterings. Poor light slows growth and inhibits flowering. Northern gardeners should be sure to fertilize and water properly during the summer to expedite the development of flowers and fruit, because this is when your plants will grow most actively.

Pineapple plants can be grown tight in the pot, fruiting in an 8- to 10-inch container. However, if a larger fruit is desired, allow the plant to reach full size by potting it in a 12-inch container. A plant with leaves that spread 2 feet wide and reach 2 feet tall is considered large.

Many pineapple varieties have leaves with sharp spines and must be approached with caution. The varieties listed here make excellent houseplants because they have spineless leaves — a distinct advantage for plants that you'll be growing inside your home!

'Royale' is modest in size and produces a sweet 1-pound fruit. The leaves have a dark band through the center.

'Smooth Cayenne' is a commercial variety that is well suited for container culture. It will produce a standard-sized pineapple like those found at grocery stores.

Size and form
2–3 feet with pruning; shrub

Bloom season
Year-round

Fruiting season
Year-round

Family
Rutaceae

Origin
Australia

Pineapple

This young pineapple needs to reach full size and turn from green to golden in color before it's ready to be picked.

The Apple/Pineapple Connection

If you'd like to speed up the fruiting process of your pineapple plant, try this amazing but effective trick: Cut a slice of apple and tuck it into the crown of your pineapple plant. The apple slice will give off enough ethylene gas to stimulate early fruiting of your pineapple plant.

Growing Conditions

Light: Full sun

Soil: Well-drained potting mix

Minimum indoor temperature: 60°F (15°C)

Hardiness outdoors: Zone 10; protect from frost

Care

Fertilizing: Apply a balanced fertilizer weekly during the active growing season.

Pruning: After harvest, when new growth has emerged from the base, remove any old growth above the new shoot by cutting it off with a knife.

Potential Problems

Pests: Not susceptible

Foliar disease: Not susceptible as long as temperatures are kept above 60°F (15°C)

Root disease: Susceptible if overwatered and in cool soil; allow soil to dry between waterings

Propagating Pineapples

Pineapple plants are easy to grow. You can start them from the green tops of grocery store pineapples, or you can buy a pineapple plant from a specialty grower. Once a plant has fruited and the pineapple has been harvested, side shoots will develop lower down on the stem, and you can work with these side shoots as well.

Planting a pineapple top (the top of the fruit with the connected leaves) is simple. Fill a small pot with potting mix and place the plant top in the pot. Make sure that the base is covered by at least 1 inch of soil. Thoroughly water and then allow the potting medium to dry between waterings. Roots will form after one to two months. Or leave the side shoots intact, and in time they will become central leaders, each of which will produce another fruit.

Pineapple Guava

Feijoa sellowiana, renamed *Acca sellowiana*

fuh-ZHOE-ah (AK-uh) sel-lo-wee-AY-nuh

Plant Particulars

Size and form
4–7 feet with pruning; upright, open shrub

Bloom season
Spring

Fruiting season
Fall

Family
Myrtaceae

Origin
Brazil, Argentina, Paraguay, and Uruguay

A drought-tolerant plant that will fruit and flower in partial sun, pineapple guava is a satisfying choice for container gardeners. With its leathery grayish-hued leaves, it will fit into any home gardening decor even before its fruit and flowers begin to appear. Pineapple guava bears beautiful flowers with sweet edible petals in spring, which are followed by oval plum-sized fruits that ripen in the fall. If you decide to eat the flowers, be sure to pick the petals only and leave the rest intact for pollination. To ensure pollination, rub your hand across the flowers before you pick off the petals.

The waxy-skinned fruit remains green even when ready for harvesting. To check for ripeness, gently squeeze the fruit. Softness is a sure sign of ripeness. A delightful fragrance is present even before the fruit is ripe. Split the fruit and scoop out the sweet, succulent, grainy flesh, which has a texture similar to a pear. The flavor hints of mint but has strong overtones of pineapple and guava. You can eat a pineapple guava like an apple, too, but we don't like to eat the sour skin. Some people, though, enjoy the unique, contradictory combination of sweet and sour.

Plants grown from seed may take two to three years to flower and fruit. On occasion seedlings need cross-pollination; grow two seedlings to ensure fruit set. If grown from a cutting or graft of a named variety, plants are guaranteed to be self-fertile and only one plant is needed.

Pineapple guava needs a chilling period to flower successfully. During the fall and winter, temperatures in the growing area need to drop down to 35–40°F (2–4°C) at night for at least two months. In the North, place plants in a garage, enclosed porch, cold sunroom, or greenhouse for this cold period. If grown outside in the ground, plants can tolerate temperatures that dip into the teens.

Pineapple guava

Pineapple guava fruits remain green even when ripe. Gently squeeze a fruit to test. If it's slightly soft, it's ready to eat.

ABOVE RIGHT: You can pick and eat the petals of pineapple guava flowers, too.

Growing Conditions

Light: Full to partial sun

Soil: Well-drained potting mix

Minimum indoor temperature: 35°F (2°C)

Hardiness outdoors: Zone 8

Care

Fertilizing: Moderate feeders; fertilize every other week during the growing season, and discontinue in late summer to allow growth to harden off. The leaves are sensitive to high fertilizer levels and can experience leaf burn.

Pruning: Young plants need frequent pruning to encourage a full, dense form. Prune back dominant vertical branches of mature plants after flowering to control size and encourage lateral branching. Avoid late summer pruning, because new buds form at this time.

Potential Problems

Pests: Not susceptible

Foliar disease: Not susceptible

Root disease: Not susceptible

Rose Apple

Syzygium jambos

siz-ZYE-gee-um JAM-bos

Drought tolerant and easy to grow, rose apple trees are suited to a home environment with low humidity and occasional dryness. They bear tasty fruit that is firm and has sweet hints of rose. The yellow fruit is oblong and hollow with a seed or two that rolls around inside.

Although a robust grower, rose apple needs to reach 4–6 feet tall before blooming begins. Plants propagated from rooted cuttings take three to four years to begin flowering and eventually need to be transplanted into a 14- to 16-inch pot. If grown from seed, the time frame is longer, but eventually seed-grown plants will reach the same mature size as plants propagated from cuttings. Flowers appear in the spring over several weeks and have a fruity fragrance.

Rose apple trees are subject to tip burn, especially when high fertilizer applications are combined with dry conditions. Tip burn looks unsightly, but it will not cause plants to die. (See page 152 for more information.)

Plant Particulars

Size and form
5–7 feet with pruning; upright tree

Bloom season
Spring

Fruiting season
Summer

Family
Myrtaceae

Origin
Southeast Asia

Rose apple

Growing Conditions

Light: Full to partial sun

Soil: Well-drained potting mix

Minimum indoor temperature: 35°F (2°C)

Hardiness outdoors: Zone 10

Care

Fertilizing: Moderate feeder; apply a balanced fertilizer weekly or every other week. Cut back in winter.

Pruning: Prune regularly to maintain height and shape. Severe pruning will reduce flowering, but selective pruning of outreaching branches can be done at any time. Flowers emerge at the tips of the previous season's growth, so heading cuts are best done in early spring.

Potential Problems

Pests: Mealybugs

Foliar disease: Few problems

Root disease: Not susceptible

The flowering sprays of rose apple are a prelude to the delicious fruit.

ABOVE: Rose apple fruits have a flavor reminiscent of rose water.

Sapodilla

Manilkara zapota

man-il-KARR-uh zuh-POH-tuh

Sapodilla fruit is commonly found in tropical markets, but it's rarely shipped north because once ripe, its soft, sweet insides don't travel well. In the wild, sapodilla plants stretch skyward to become 30-foot trees. These trees are also famous as a source of natural latex, known as chicle — the material chewing gum is made from.

Sapodilla fruit takes many months to grow and then ripen. Once the fruit has reached a mature size, it will hold on the branches for several months until it becomes soft and ready for picking. The outer skin is light brown and remains light brown when ripe. Cut ripe fruits in half and scrape out the flesh with a spoon. The flavor is sweet and reminiscent of brown sugar. The inner fruit is light tan. Hand-pollination is helpful in setting fruit when plants are grown indoors; see page 134 for more information.

'Silas Woods' is an exceptional dwarf cultivar that produces fruit when young, often within the first year as a container plant. And 'Silas Woods' is well suited for pot culture because its sprawling growth can be maintained at less than 5 feet in height. A plant in an 8-inch pot can produce 10 to 15 fruits each year.

Size and form
3–5 feet with pruning; sprawling tree

Bloom season
Possibly year-round, usually late winter to early summer

Fruiting season
Usually 6–10 months after flowering

Family
Sapotaceae

Origin
Central America

'Silas Woods' sapodilla

The custardlike pulp inside sapodilla fruits has a delectable brown sugar flavor.

Growing Conditions

Light: Full sun

Soil: Well-drained potting mix

Minimum indoor temperature: 60°F (15°C); tolerates temperatures down to 35°F (2°C) for short periods

Hardiness outdoors: Zone 10

Care

Fertilizing: Moderate feeders; apply a balanced fertilizer weekly during the growing season. Discontinue when growth slows (usually during winter).

Pruning: Prune as needed to control size once fruit has been harvested.

Potential Problems

Pests: Mealybugs

Foliar disease: Not susceptible

Root disease: Not susceptible

Star Fruit

Averrhoa carambola

av-er-ROH-ah kah-rahm-BOH-luh

Plant Particulars

Size and form
4–5 feet with pruning; multi-stemmed tree

Bloom season
Intermittently year-round

Fruiting season
Summer, fall, and winter

Family
Oxalidaceae

Origin
Southeast Asia and Malaysia

Star fruit is an enchanting tropical tree known for its prolific sweet fruit that has an attractive five-pointed star shape. On some varieties, fruits can grow up to 4 inches across and 7 inches long. When the fruit is sliced, the thin yellow outer skin outlines paler, sweet flesh. Also known as carambola, it is loaded with antioxidants and flavonoids and has only about 30 calories per fruit. In its native regions, this upright tree grows 20–30 feet tall, and one tree has been known to feed a whole village.

As a potted specimen, star fruit will begin bearing at 3–4 feet for standard varieties and at less than 2 feet for dwarf varieties. The foliage is compound, which means that each leaf stem is clothed with five to ten small, oval leaves. Small clusters of lilac-colored flowers bloom several times a year on old woody growth as well as on mature young branches. In the North, move the plants outside in the summer for insect pollination since it's the summer blooms that produce the most fruit. Whether indoors or out, warm temperatures (high 70s and 80s [24–32°C]) and direct sunlight are needed to promote fruit set. Failure to set fruit is generally caused by a combination of cool temperatures and low light.

'Sri Kembangan' is a full-size tree that produces excellent-quality sweet fruit that ripens to a golden orange. Plants can be maintained at 4–6 feet in containers.

'Hart' and 'Dwarf Hawaiian' are medium-sized varieties that grow well in containers. They produce sweet, pale yellow fruit and can be maintained at 3–4 feet.

'Dwarf Maher' is one of the best varieties for container culture. It will fruit when less than 2 feet tall and can be maintained at less than 3 feet. It's an amazing producer of 3- to 4-inch-long fruit. In 2009, we kept our 'Dwarf Maher' in a greenhouse for warmth, and it set fruit much better than the other star fruits, which were left outside in what was an unusually cool — and decidedly nontropical — New England summer.

'Dwarf Maher' star fruit

Recipes from the Tropical Kitchen

Star Fruit Snack

Try this if you are looking for a healthy snack full of anti-oxidants, flavonoids, and vitamin C with very little sugar.

1	cup sugar
1	cup water
2–3	star fruits, thinly sliced

In a medium saucepan, combine the sugar and water. Bring to a boil, and remove from the heat. Add the star fruits and let sit 15 minutes. Preheat the oven to 200°F. Line a half sheet pan (11 by 17 inches) with a nonstick baking mat or parchment paper. Remove the star fruit slices from the syrup one at a time and arrange in a single layer on the baking sheet. Bake for 1 hour, or until dry. Cool on a rack and enjoy as a healthy snack. Store the dried fruit in an airtight container.

Makes 15 to 24 slices

Star Fruit, Pineapple, and Mango Salsa

Star fruit, pineapple, and mango make this a truly tropical dish. This salsa is as beautiful to look at as it is delicious to eat. The taste alone transports you to a tropical paradise. And on top of all that, this fabulous salsa is low in calories, too!

1	cup diced star fruit
1	cup peeled and diced mango
½	cup peeled and diced pineapple
¼	cup diced red bell pepper
¼	cup diced red onion
2	tablespoons chopped fresh mint leaves
2	tablespoons fresh lime juice

Combine all ingredients. Chill. Serve with pork, chicken, or fish.

Makes about 3 cups

LEFT: The long, slender fruits of 'Dwarf Maher' star fruit form as soon as the plant attains a height of 2 feet.

TOP RIGHT: Plump fruits grace the branches of a 'Sri Kembangan' star fruit, a vigorous tree that can be kept at 4–6 feet tall when grown in a container.

Growing Conditions

Light: Full sun

Soil: Well-drained potting mix

Minimum indoor temperature: 55°F (13°C)

Hardiness outdoors: Zone 9

Care

Fertilizing: Moderate feeders; fertilize weekly or every other week from late winter through fall. Reduce frequency or stop when not in active growth.

Pruning: When plants are young, prune back upright branches to promote a multi-stemmed bushy specimen; prune overly long branches at any time to maintain size and form.

Potential Problems

Pests: Aphids, especially with high fertility; spider mites in hot, dry conditions

Foliar disease: Not susceptible

Root disease: Not susceptible

Tree Tomato

Cyphomandra crassicaulis

sy-foh-MAN-druh crass-ih-CAW-lus

Plant Particulars

Size and form
3–5 feet with pruning; bush or small tree

Bloom season
Spring, summer, and fall

Fruiting season
Fall through winter; fruit can ripen intermittently year-round

Family
Solanaceae

Origin
Andes Mountains

lusters of deep mahogany-red fruit dangle from the tree tomato, also called tamarillo. This pleasing ornamental display appears just in time for the winter holiday season. Not just pretty to look at, the egg-shaped, egg-sized fruit is delightfully tangy. Just cut the fruit in half and scoop out the flesh in cantaloupe-like fashion.

Tree tomato is a fast grower that is as foolproof as its cousin, the garden tomato. The large leaves have a pungent odor, and clusters of fragrant flowers cover the leaf axils. In the North, plants begin flowering in early spring and continue to fruit into late summer. The fruits of summer will hold on in clusters of two or three and ripen from fall into the short dark days of winter; the fruit is ready to eat when fully red.

Cutting-grown plants are best for containers, especially if growing space is limited. Seed-grown plants take longer to mature to fruiting size. Even young cuttings in 3- or 4-inch pots will flower and fruit. To keep the plant small and contained yet productive, pot your tree tomato in an 8- to 10-inch container. For a 4- to 6-foot tree, transplant it into a 14- to 16-inch pot.

Plants will tolerate cold nighttime temperatures as long as they are kept above freezing, or for safety's sake, 35°F (2°C). To winter over, keep the tree tomato in a cold greenhouse, sunroom, or any sunny area with temperatures above 35°F (2°C). Plants that don't receive sufficient light will become leggy.

Tree tomato

Tree tomato offers an enticing display of mahogany-colored egg-shaped fruit from summer through midwinter.

TOP RIGHT: To eat a ripe fruit, scoop out the insides, including the seeds, and enjoy the sweet custard.

Growing Conditions

Light: Full to partial sun

Soil: Well-drained potting mix

Minimum indoor temperature: 35°F (2°C)

Hardiness outdoors: Zone 10; Zone 9 with protection

Care

Fertilizing: Heavy feeder; apply a balanced fertilizer weekly or every other week when temperatures are above 60°F (15°C). Reduce or stop in winter.

Pruning: Prune after harvest in late winter to control size; plants can withstand severe pruning and will quickly resprout, even on old woody stems. Plants can even be cut back to a leafless stem to restructure plant form. Additional pruning can be done anytime growth is excessive; make cuts high on the plant, above the level where fruit has formed.

Potential Problems

Pests: Whiteflies and aphids

Foliar disease: Susceptible to leaf spot diseases in wet conditions with poor air circulation

Root disease: Susceptible when in cold, wet soil

 **Egg Count**

The rich mahogany color of a tree tomato "egg" could rival the beauty of a precious Fabergé egg, but the thing that makes this plant so special in our family history was the annual tradition of counting the ripe eggs. Every fall, Joy (Byron's mother) and her brother Richard Logee would place bets on how many eggs would ripen on the tree tomato tree. However, we don't know if anyone ever really won the bet, because before the count could be confirmed, ripened eggs would mysteriously appear in a wooden bowl in Joy's kitchen, waiting to be consumed. And Uncle Richard would be left scratching his head, wondering if he miscounted.

chocolate

coffee

yerba maté

tea

3 Coffee, Tea, and Chocolate

Chocolate · Coffee
Tea · Yerba Maté

Chocolate

Theobroma cacao

thee-oh-BRO-mah kah-KOW

Plant Particulars

Size and form
5–6 feet with pruning; upright tree

Bloom season
Year-round

Fruiting season
Year-round

Family
Sterculiaceae

Origin
Andes Mountains

𝓜ost of us love chocolate. But even if you don't, it's exciting to grow your own cocoa pods. Like a scene out of *Charlie and the Chocolate Factory,* when looking at your lovely fruiting chocolate plant, you almost expect to see an Oompa-Loompa appear and snatch the large ribbed yellow pods from the tree. You'll need to be patient, though, because plants take several years to bloom, and flowering can occur for up to a year before fruit sets.

Chocolate makes an excellent container plant as long as it has enough space to mature. In its native habitat, chocolate is an understory plant that grows beneath large trees, so it tolerates partial shade. It benefits from some direct sunlight. Generally, a chocolate plant needs to grow close to 5 feet tall before flowering; the trunk will become woody and the plant will fork, creating two separate leads from the central stem. This can take up to three years. Flower buds and then pods appear along the trunk.

When given warmth, fertilizer, and good light, chocolate is a fast grower. Place outside in the summer to allow insect pollination; hand-pollination is helpful to ensure fruit set. (See Pollinating Plants by Hand, page 134.) The pods change color from green to yellow or red when ripe, depending on the variety. In our experience, the small yellow-podded type is the earliest to flower and fruit.

Watch for brown edges on older leaves. This may occur under cooler, slower growing conditions. Although cosmetically unappealing, the discoloration is not harmful. Fruit production and plant health remain normal.

Chocolate

Converting Cacao Pods to Chocolate Nibs

Getting chocolate from your plants requires fermentation. It's a fairly simple process. Here's how to do it:

1. Split yellow ripe cocoa (*cacao*) pods in half. Use at least six pods; the more pods the better, because a larger mass of beans promotes better fermentation.

2. Remove the raw cocoa beans (leave the husk on) from the pods; the beans are about the size of a quarter and will come out easily.

3. Puncture the bottom of an upright plastic quart container in three or four places for drainage holes. Fill with the cocoa beans and cover with a double layer of cheesecloth secured with a rubber band so fruit flies cannot enter.

4. Let the container sit at room temperature for about a week; the beans will ferment as they sit.

5. Rinse the beans with cool water and spread out in a single layer to dry.

The husk on the beans will turn light brown as it dries; this can take a week or more.

6. At the end of the week, spread the beans on a baking sheet in a single layer and place in an oven at the lowest setting for about 30 minutes to ensure dryness.

7. Remove the husks from the beans. The husks should rub off easily in your hands, and then you can break the cocoa beans into bits called nibs.

Chocolate nibs are not sweet but are filled with antioxidants. Try adding them to cottage cheese or yogurt or mix them with raisins or goji berries for a healthy snack. For a natural chocolate confection, soak them in maple syrup and dry on a cookie sheet in a warm oven. Or if you want to supply healthy flair to an indulgent treat, add the nibs to a batch of brownies for an enhanced chocolate flavor and a satisfying crunch.

Growing Conditions

Light: Full to partial sun

Soil: Well-drained potting mix

Minimum indoor temperature: For best growth, keep above 60°F (15°C); tolerates lower temperatures for short periods

Hardiness outdoors: Zone 10

Care

Fertilizing: Moderate feeder; add a balanced fertilizer to the container every week or two year-round when grown in warm conditions.

Pruning: Once plants begin producing flowers, prune anytime a plant is too large or unruly. Since flowering occurs on old wood, head back branches only as needed to maintain the form of the plant.

Potential Problems

Pests: Aphids and mealybugs

Foliar disease: Few problems outside the tropics

Root disease: Susceptible in cold, wet conditions

Ripe cocoa pods.

TOP RIGHT: Inside a cocoa pod, nature wraps each cocoa bean inside its own white husk. These husks happen to be edible — and sweet!

photograph © Richard Wallace

Coffee

Coffea arabica

KOF-fee-uh uh-RAB-ih-kuh

rinking coffee can be addictive, and once you start growing and harvesting your own coffee beans, there's no doubt you'll be hooked for life. Fragrant flowers and clusters of colorful fruit make coffee a great plant for the container gardener. Flowers and fruits appear when the plant is young, often when only 3–4 feet tall. Under ideal growing conditions, this can happen in less than a year.

Coffee plants adapt well to the low light and low humidity typical of home environments. Their growth habit is like that of a Christmas tree, with a central leader and lateral branches. Plants increase in height quickly, and they also slowly grow wider over time.

Clusters of fragrant white flowers form on the lateral branches but are short-lived, lasting only a day or two. The coffee fruits follow the flowers, appearing first as green berries that eventually ripen to red. Once a good amount of fruit has set, blooming nearly comes to a halt, but plants will rebloom on new growth. The berries are ready to pick and harvest when cherry red.

We have friends who have nurtured their coffee plant over the past three years from a baby in a 2½-inch pot into a healthy, full-fruiting specimen with shiny green leaves in a 14-inch pot. It stands over 6 feet tall. They have become so enamored with their coffee plant that they call it "Maxwell."

Indoors in the low light of winter, coffee leaves can brown at the edges, especially older leaves. Excessive fertilizer or disease can also cause brown leaf edges. If moving the plant to a spot with more light doesn't correct the problem, see page 152 for more remedies.

Plant Particulars

Size and form
5–6 feet; upright tree

Bloom season
Intermittently year-round; heaviest flowering in late winter and spring

Fruiting season
Year-round; heaviest fruiting from fall into winter

Family
Rubiaceae

Origin
Ethiopia and Yemen

Coffee

First Cup of Coffee: How to Harvest, Dry, and Roast Your Own Beans

A coffee tree will ordinarily take three to four years before it produces enough fruit for a real crop of coffee "cherries" or beans.

Harvesting

Fruit is ripe and ready to be picked when it has turned from green to pure red. Pick only the red cherries; the green ones will produce bitter coffee. Rinse the cherries well.

Drying

Remove most of the skin and pulp by rolling a rolling pin forcefully back and forth over the cherries. The beans will slide out, still covered with some pulp and a thin layer called the parchment. Put beans in a container and fill with water. Ripe beans will sink; unripe or bad beans will float. Remove the floating beans.

Put beans in a plastic container and fill with fresh water to cover. Put a lid on the container and let the beans soak for one or two days. Check a handful of beans occasionally. If they are still slick and smooth, let them continue soaking; if rough and bumpy or grainy they are ready to be drained and dried.

Spread out the beans in a thin layer on a wire rack. Move the rack to a place with good indirect light for several days, and then into full sun. Stir the beans at least three times daily to promote even drying and prevent mildew. Depending on humidity and temperature, it will take 5 to 15 days for the beans to dry. When they're ready, the parchment will be crumbly and easy to remove by rubbing the beans firmly between your palms. Dry beans can be stored for up to one year before roasting.

Roasting

Using a hot-air popcorn popper with a solid bottom (no air intake vents on the bottom of the machine) and side vents, you can roast beans in 4 to 6 minutes. Follow the popper instructions regarding quantity, substituting beans for corn kernels. Turn on the machine, and then listen for the first "crack" of the dry beans. A fine coating on the bean, called chaff, will be blown off and out of the popper. Watch carefully, and remove the beans when they are slightly less dark than you would like — they continue to cook after they are removed from the popper. To quickly cool them, pour them from one colander to another, or stir them in a colander with a wooden spoon. If not quickly cooled, they will make a flat-tasting cup of coffee. Let the beans sit out for 12 hours after roasting to allow any excess gas to evaporate, and then store in an airtight glass container. To enjoy the beans at peak flavor, grind and brew into coffee within one to three days after roasting.

You can roast small amounts of coffee beans in a popcorn popper, a heavy-duty pan or wok, or a pan in the oven.

Growing Conditions

Light: Full to partial sun; will grow and flower in partial sun

Soil: Well-drained potting mix

Minimum indoor temperature: 40°F (4°C); tolerates short periods of colder temperatures but not freezing

Hardiness outdoors: Zone 10; protect from freezing

Care

Fertilizing: Moderate feeder; apply fertilizer weekly during spring through summer. Discontinue in fall and winter.

Pruning: Cut back tops when plants outgrow their growing area, reducing height by 1–3 feet. A coffee plant cut to half its size will resprout in no time.

Potential Problems

Pests: Highly susceptible to mealybugs

Foliar disease: Occasional problems

Root disease: Not susceptible; strong root system

Tea

Camellia sinensis

cuh-MEE-lee-uh sy-NEN-sis

Large showy blooms and fragrance are hallmarks of many types of camellias, but this species is known for its leaves — tea leaves. The plant does offer pretty white or pink blossoms, and it makes a great potted plant that is easy to grow when given the proper conditions. Camellias prefer a cool growing area in the winter for bud development. But if your goal is to produce tea leaves rather than flowers, then the warmer temperature of a typical home during the winter is a plus — plants grow best when temperatures are above 60°F (15°C). Brown leaf edges are a common sign of overfertilization; see page 152 for treatment advice for this problem.

This species grows faster than other camellias, which are typically slow growers. If temperatures are warm, plants put out two or more flushes of new growth a year. Tea leaves are harvested from the young shoots, so once the plant reaches the size you would like, you can harvest twice a year. The tea leaves are generally dried for a mellower flavor. Fresh leaves can be used, but the strong taste is not as palatable even for the most faithful tea drinkers.

Plant Particulars

Size and form
3–5 feet; shrub

Bloom season
Spring

Fruiting season
Grown for its leaves

Family
Theaceae

Origin
Southeast Asia

Tea

The tender juvenile leaves of the tea plant are highly sought after to make a less acidic and delicious tea known as "white tea."

Growing Conditions

Light: Partial sun

Soil: Well-drained acidic potting mix (half sphagnum peat and half perlite)

Minimum indoor temperature: 30°F (−1°C)

Hardiness outdoors: Zone 8

Care

Fertilizing: Light feeder; begin fertilizing once a month in late winter or spring when new growth has just begun. Stop by late summer to allow growth to harden off. Never apply full-strength fertilizer; always dilute first. Never apply when soil is dry.

Pruning: Cut back main shoots of young plants to promote a multi-stemmed form. In late winter before growth starts, prune older plants as needed to maintain size. Harvest leaves by snipping shoots as needed.

Potential Problems

Pests: Not susceptible

Foliar disease: Not susceptible

Root disease: Susceptible under damp, cool conditions and high soil nutrient levels. Use a well-drained potting mix and allow soil to dry a little between waterings.

Yerba Maté

Ilex paraguariensis

EYE-lex par-uh-gwar-ee-EN-sis

Yerba maté, made from the leaves and stems of *Ilex paraguariensis*, is the beverage of choice in South America. Maté bars in South America are like North American coffee bars. Maté drinks can be ordered sweetened or unsweetened, foamed, frothed, roasted, or toasted; the choice is yours.

When it comes to growing yerba maté (also called cup herb or Paraguay tea), it is important to allow plants to become well established before harvesting too many of the leaves and stems for tea. While waiting for plants to mature, enjoy the graceful full-leafed branches, which cover themselves with tiny white flowers from winter through spring. Flowering may continue sporadically into summer.

Give yerba maté a warm, sunny spot above 60°F (15°C), with moderate amounts of fertilizer for fast growth. Once plants are established, they are vigorous growers, especially during the long days of summer. Yerba maté can fit into a variety of growing spaces. For a windowsill, you can grow it in a 6- to 8-inch pot and keep it well pruned. Or give it a 14- to 16-inch pot and allow it to become a 6- to 8-foot-tall shrub for a conservatory or sunroom.

Size and form
2–8 feet with pruning; shrub or tree

Bloom season
Late winter and spring

Fruiting season
Grown for its leaves

Family
Aquifoliaceae

Origin
South America

Yerba maté

Flowers form on the flush of new green growth on maté plants in late winter and spring. The mature dark green leaves are harvested for tea.

Growing Conditions

Light: Full to partial sun

Soil: Well-drained potting mix

Minimum indoor temperature: 50°F (10°C); can tolerate temperatures just above freezing for short periods

Hardiness outdoors: Zone 9

Care

Fertilizing: Moderate feeders; fertilize every two weeks with a dilute balanced fertilizer. If temperatures remain above 60°F (15°C), feed year-round.

Pruning: Prune when young to create a dense, multi-stemmed specimen. Once mature, prune plants periodically to curb branches that stretch out too far, to maintain size overall, and to increase shoot production.

Potential Problems

Pests: Few problems

Foliar disease: Few problems

Root disease: Few problems

 ## A Perfect Cup of Maté Tea

Maté tea has all the antioxidant properties of green tea, as well as plenty of caffeine. Mature leaves and stems make the best tea. You can identify mature leaves by their texture and color. They are stiffer and darker in color than the soft light green of the young juvenile growth. Harvest mature leaves and stems at any time of the year. Put in an airy spot out of direct sunlight to dry. (Arranging the stems on a dish-drying rack works well.) When the leaves are dry enough to crumble easily, remove them from the stems and break or cut the stems into small pieces. Crush the stems and leaves with a mortar and pestle for a finer tea. Pour 1 cup hot (but not boiling) water over 1 tablespoon maté and steep for 5 minutes. Strain the tea and enjoy.

vanilla

sugarcane

black pepper

cinnamon

Sugar and Spices

4

Black Pepper
Cinnamon
Sugarcane
Vanilla

Black Pepper

Piper nigrum

PY-per NY-grum

Well-known spice for thousands of years, pepper is also an excellent container plant for gardeners everywhere. After several years, plants grown in pots produce an abundance of peppercorns. Under good growing conditions, peppers fruit most of the year, usually hesitating for a month or two in the winter when light levels are low. The peppercorns appear as small green beads clustered along the flower stems. They are ready to pick when the oldest peppercorns on the stem begin to turn red. See Pepper Processing Procedures on page 117 to learn how to harvest four different colors of peppercorns from a single plant.

A unique feature of this vine is the small crystalline balls that form on leaf undersides and stems. These are a harmless fluid containing sugars (called exudates); over time, these balls turn black. You might think they are insect eggs or insects, but don't try to remove them. They are not harmful to the plant and are part of the plant's normal physiology.

Make sure you buy a pepper plant that has been propagated from a fruiting plant, because some clones never produce fruit. Although a somewhat slow grower, this vining plant needs some support. Plants grow best when grown tight in their pots (slightly potbound); do not put into too large a pot. Plants can be maintained easily in 6- to 8-inch pots.

Plant Particulars

Size and form
2–3 feet with support and pruning; woody vine

Bloom season
Year-round; bloom is heaviest during warm weather

Fruiting season
Year-round

Family
Piperaceae

Origin
Southern India

Black pepper

Dangling chains of red ripe pepper-corns can be found year-round on a potted black pepper plant.

Growing Conditions

Light: Partial sun to shade; some direct sunlight helps increase flowering

Soil: Well-drained potting mix

Minimum indoor temperature: 60°F (15°C), preferably 65°F (18°C); grows best when temperatures are above 70°F (21°C)

Hardiness outdoors: Zone 10; does not tolerate freezing

Care

Fertilizing: Moderate feeders; apply a balanced fertilizer once a month when actively growing, usually spring to fall. Plants are sensitive to high salt levels.

Pruning: Prune in late winter or early spring, just as active growth begins in earnest. To control height, prune plants lightly or wrap vining stems around a support, such as wire hoops or stakes.

Potential Problems

Pests: Mealybugs

Foliar disease: Not susceptible

Root disease: Can be a problem in containers. Grow in a terra-cotta pot and use a fast-draining potting mix; keep in a warm environment and allow soil to dry out between waterings. Go easy on the fertilizer.

⊙→ Pepper Processing Procedures

By selecting the time of harvest and the method of processing, you can harvest all four types of peppercorns (black, white, green, and red) from one plant. Different processing is needed to preserve each stage of the peppercorn. For example, green (unripe) peppercorns are highly perishable once picked. Sections of cut stalk with the green peppercorns still attached need to be immersed in brine in a container such as a 12-ounce canning jar. Make the brine by combining 8 ounces vinegar (or water) with 2 teaspoons salt.

Final color	When to harvest	Processing method
Black	While still unripe (green)	Scald in hot water; dry in a single layer
White	When ripe (red)	Remove skin; dry in a single layer
Green	While still unripe (green)	Put in brine
Red	When ripe (red)	Dry; preserve in brine

Cinnamon

Cinnamomum zeylanicum

sin-uh-MOH-mum zey-LAN-ee-kum

Cinnamon is well known for its culinary uses, yet it is hardly ever grown in ordinary home settings. It's easy to grow, however. As long as the soil is kept slightly dry, a potted cinnamon plant can thrive for years without special care. You can keep the plants as small as 3 feet by pruning regularly, or you can repot them over time into a 12- to 14-inch pot and allow them to reach up to 8 feet tall.

The leathery, rich reddish bronze juvenile growth provides a nice contrast to the dark green mature leaves. (However, mature leaves will remain light green if plants are kept in high light.) Sprays of small white flowers appear in summer. The purplish black berries are inedible; it's the bark that is harvested for its culinary qualities.

Both the stem and bark are highly aromatic, and it's the inner bark that is used as a spice. Even small stems can be scratched to release a rich cinnamon fragrance. True cinnamon is often confused with cassia, also known as Chinese or Vietnamese cinnamon (*Cinnamomum cassia*). Although the latter is more common in the United States as a spice and is often offered for sale as true cinnamon, it's not as aromatic, and it has a stronger, more assertive flavor. True cinnamon (*C. zeylanicum)* can be grown from seed, vegetative cuttings, or grafts, but it is more difficult to propagate vegetatively than cassia.

On occasion, cinnamon produces seeds, which can be picked and planted. These seeds must be picked when ripe (black in color) and planted right away because seed viability is limited.

Plant Particulars

Size and form
3–8 feet depending on pruning and container size; shrub

Bloom season
Spring to summer

Fruiting season
Grown for its bark

Family
Lauraceae

Origin
Sri Lanka, Madagascar, and southwest India

Cinnamon

Harvesting Cinnamon Sticks

Cinnamon sticks are simply dried bark from a mature cinnamon plant; you can easily harvest your own. Commercial cinnamon is cut into uniform lengths and graded according to thickness, aroma, and appearance. Stems are continually cut back to stimulate new stem growth for harvesting. Some recipes call for mature wood; others call for young whips (stems). We like using the young whips because they are more fragrant and seem to hold their aromatic properties better than the older wood. Try both to see which you prefer.

Harvesting bark from young whips. Cut the whips into 3-inch segments. Score the bark lengthwise from end to end, cutting just deep enough to loosen the bark. Peel off the bark, which will naturally curl. Dry in an open, airy, warm spot such as on a kitchen counter. For a thicker, compact stick, layer the bark pieces inside one another before drying. Once dried, the sticks can be shaved for the spice or used in a mulling mix.

Harvesting outer bark of mature wood. Cut stems into 3-inch segments. Make a lengthwise slice halfway into the stem, but do not go all the way through. The bark will not peel as easily as it does from a younger stem. Instead, scrape out the core and pithy inner lining, then allow the remaining bark to dry completely. You can layer several pieces of bark together to produce a thicker stick called a quill.

Growing Conditions

Light: Full to partial sun

Soil: Well-drained, acidic potting mix (half sphagnum moss and half perlite)

Minimum indoor temperature: 60°F (15°C)

Hardiness outdoors: Zone 10; protect from frost

Care

Fertilizing: Moderate feeder; fertilize weekly or biweekly, but only during active growth (late winter until fall).

Pruning: Prune at any time for harvest or to prevent plants from becoming too tall or wide.

Potential Problems

Pests: Mealybugs

Foliar disease: Not susceptible; leaf edges turn brown if salt (fertilizer) levels get too high

Root disease: Susceptible to root rot if not kept on the dry side

Young leaves of cinnamon plants have an attractive reddish bronze coloration.

Sugarcane

Saccharum officinarum

SAK-ker-um off-ih-kih-NAY-rum

Watching a small sugarcane plant that started out in a 2½-inch pot grow into a giant 6-foot specimen in one summer is reward enough, but for us the pleasure increases when our children's faces light up at the announcement of the harvest. It's no longer just a family tradition but a neighborhood tradition, and everyone gathers to harvest his or her own cane (stem).

Sugarcane can be grown in a wide variety of conditions including cool temperatures and moderate light. Providing warmth, lots of sunlight, and copious amounts of water and fertilizer will encourage fast growth. When this grass is mature (it will reach 5 to 6 feet tall when grown in a 12- to 16-inch pot), white flowering plumes appear.

Black-stemmed sugarcane

Black-stemmed sugarcane is identical to commercial sugarcane except that its mature stems are black. It makes a dramatic statement for the home gardener and brings an Eastern design element to the home. As it grows, the older leaves fall off and the dark black stems remain. Over time the canes will grow to 1½ inches in diameter. For a big sugar treat, wait two seasons or more to harvest, until the cane diameter is 3–4 inches (the larger the cane, the sweeter the cane). Black-stemmed sugarcane is slow growing; in the North it needs a few seasons for the canes to reach a good size. The leaf edges of this sugarcane are sharp and spiny; it requires caution to tend and harvest.

Red-stemmed sugarcane

Red-stemmed sugarcane (*S. officinarum purpurea*) has purple-toned leaves and stems. Its fountainlike spray of long leaves is easier to handle than that of the commercial species. The leaves are not as spiny as those of black-stemmed sugarcane. Its fast-growing stature fits well in the summer garden, whether planted in the ground or in pots. The canes mature in one season. Although somewhat slender, they contain sweet juices just like the stockier black-stemmed variety.

Plant Particulars

Size and form
5–6 feet; perennial grass

Bloom season
Variable

Fruiting season
Variable (seeds will ripen as soon as stems mature)

Family
Poaceae

Origin
Southeast Asia

Red-stemmed sugarcane

Black-stemmed sugarcane, which has bright green leaves, is closely related to commercial sugarcane.

Red-stemmed sugarcane is used as an ornamental, but it will also reward you with sweet canes.

TOP RIGHT: The stems of black-stemmed sugarcane have shorter segments (internodes) than those of red-stemmed sugarcane.

Growing Conditions

Light: Full sun

Soil: Well-drained potting mix

Minimum indoor temperature: 40°F (4°C)

Hardiness outdoors: Zone 10

Care

Fertilizing: Fertilize weekly or biweekly as long as temperatures remain warm. Reduce or stop in winter.

Pruning: Stems (canes) can be pruned at any time. Tame unruly plants by cutting down to a foot or less above the soil.

Potential Problems

Pests: Not susceptible

Foliar disease: Can occur under wet conditions, but are only cosmetic

Root disease: Not susceptible

 # Harvesting Sugarcane

Mature canes are harvested usually when 1–2 inches in diameter. It's a simple task to peel the cane and reveal the sweet, fibrous inner stem. First cut the cane, which can be 4–5 feet long. Then cut the cane into 6-inch segments. Make a vertical cut lengthwise in each segment and the outside skin will peel away. Chew on the succulent stem and taste the world's favorite sweetener, pure sugar. The cane ripens from the bottom to the top, so the bottom of the cane is always sweeter. Sugarcane juice is squeezed from the stems, and both white sugar and brown sugar are produced from this juice.

Vanilla

Vanilla planifolia

vuh-NIL-luh plan-ih-FOH-lee-uh

anilla is the spice that bakers covet most. Countries have even gone to war over vanilla. This slow-growing vine needs support and thrives under warm, humid conditions. Like most orchids, it needs good-quality light and a healthy root system to flower and bloom. The potting mix needs to be airy and porous — sphagnum moss is a great growing medium for this epiphyte. Some support is needed so vanilla can anchor its roots and make its vertical climb. You can allow your vanilla vine to ramble over a slab of cedar or cypress, a column of cork or tree fern, or even a whole wall in a sunroom or greenhouse. Where space is an issue, grow on a trellis or hoop and wrap the vine around itself.

It takes several years of good growth to bring a young plant into flower, so patience is needed. Plants seem to flower better once the vining stems have climbed to the top of a structure and then toppled over to dangle in the air. The flowers form at the leaf axils and emerge from short stems in clusters, with individual flowers opening successively over a period of many days or even weeks. The blooms are open only one day and need to be hand-pollinated to produce beans. (See Pollinating Plants by Hand on page 134.) After pollination, the young green pods (beans) grow very fast, reaching 8–10 inches long in a few weeks. Pods then remain on the plant for up to six months before ripening.

A variegated form of vanilla has beautiful golden striped leaves, and it flowers more slowly, even when the vine is mature, mostly because variegated plants have less chlorophyll.

Plant Particulars

Size and form
5–10 feet with support; woody vine

Bloom season
Spring through fall

Fruiting season
Year-round

Family
Orchidaceae

Origin
Mexico

Variegated vanilla

Recipes from the Tropical Kitchen

Rick's Rum-Infused Vanilla Dessert

Greenhouse manager Rick Logee knows how to grow plants the Logee way! He manages and grows over 1,200 varieties of tropical plants, so it's a wonder he had time to share his favorite vanilla recipe. His wife, Deb, says that using clear Jamaican rum is a must to produce the best vanilla extract.

2	extra-large dried vanilla beans, or 4 small
1	cup clear Jamaican rum
8	ounces ricotta cheese or plain yogurt
1	teaspoon raw sugar
4–6	ounces blueberries, raspberries, or strawberries

Cut beans in half lengthwise and place in a clean 8-ounce glass container with a secure lid (the beans must fit completely inside the container). Add the rum and allow to soak for 2 months to make vanilla extract. When the extract is ready, combine ½ teaspoon of the extract with the ricotta, sugar, and fruit.

Serves 2

The vanilla flower is a small orchid that is beautiful to behold but lasts only one day.

→ How to Make Vanilla Extract

Vanilla beans take six to nine months to mature on the vine. You'll know the beans are ready to pick once they begin to turn yellow. Here's how to process your homegrown beans:

1. Pick beans when they begin to turn yellow.
2. Blanch in hot water for a few minutes (this helps clean the surfaces of mold).
3. Spread on paper towels and dry out of direct sunlight in an airy spot with low humidity. Drying takes several weeks or even a few months. Beans turn black when dry.
4. Once dried, soak 3 or 4 beans in ½ cup of vodka to make a strong, baker's-quality vanilla extract.

Growing Conditions

Light: Partial sun

Soil: Orchid potting mix or sphagnum moss

Minimum indoor temperature: 60°F (15°C)

Hardiness outdoors: Zone 10; protect from frost

Care

Fertilizing: Light feeder; supply ½ teaspoon of a balanced fertilizer every two weeks.

Pruning: Little is needed. Wrap stem back around itself to maintain size.

Potential Problems

Pests: Not susceptible

Foliar disease: Susceptible in conditions of stagnant air, wet foliage, and cool temperatures

Root disease: Susceptible if grown in a heavy potting mix or a container with poor drainage, especially in cool temperatures

A babaco, or mountain papaya,
tree in a sturdy container makes
an attractive focal point on a sunny
expanse of lawn.

Plant Care

5

Getting Started from the Bottom Up

Maintaining Your Plants

Propagation

Pests and Diseases

Troubleshooting Guide

Getting Started from the Bottom Up

Success with growing potted fruits — or any type of potted plant — starts with creating a soil environment in your pot that will support healthy roots, which in turn will support healthy foliage and fruit. Roots need water and nutrients, of course, but they also need air. When you water a potted plant, the water must be able to pass quickly through the potting mix, saturating it. If water pools in the soil for long periods of time at the bottom of a pot, roots and plants will suffer from lack of oxygen. And if drainage is poor, there's a greater risk that fertilizer salts will accumulate and burn roots, and that infection by disease organisms that thrive in wet conditions will occur.

Choosing Containers

It's fun to choose containers with unique shapes or pretty patterns, but to be safe, it's wise to evaluate a pot from the growing angle before you buy. Every pot needs drainage holes, typically in the bottom of the pot. Some pots have side drainage holes, and these pots work fine, too. In a pinch, short-term use of hole-less pots is possible but you must be accurate with your watering to avoid oversaturating the soil.

Many plants also do best if the soil is allowed to dry out between waterings. For these plants, it's important to choose a container material such as terra-cotta that "breathes," allowing moisture to escape. A drier root environment means more air exchange, which means less of an opportunity for root diseases to take hold. We believe that the terra-cotta pot, in most circumstances, is the best long-term container. Terra-cotta and unglazed clay exert a wicking action that draws water out of the potting mix and through the container sides and bottom, which helps soil dry out between waterings (though it may require watering more frequently). Our rule of thumb is this: if you tend to overwater, use terra-cotta pots; if you tend to underwater, use plastic pots. Experiment with plastic; many people grow their plants successfully in plastic with proper watering and a well-drained potting mix.

We don't use plastic self-watering containers. The reservoir of water that wicks into the soil slows the drying of the potting mix and may cause an unhealthy root environment. Self-watering plastic pots are useful for bog-type plants, but potted fruit trees and other fruiting plants need soil that dries out between waterings.

Potting Mixes

Container plants can grow reasonably well in a wide variety of soilless mixes. Choose a mix that is heavy enough to act as a substrate in which the root system can anchor itself, but porous enough to allow water to drain rapidly and air to penetrate easily.

continued on page 128

Pot Pros and Cons

Unglazed Clay/Terra-Cotta

Advantages

- Fast drainage
- Allows air to move into the soil mix
- Wicking action helps soil dry out between waterings
- Environmentally more sound than plastic

Disadvantages

- Heavy; can be hard to move
- Breakable
- Limited design and little variation in color
- Cannot winter over outside unless emptied and inverted
- More expensive than plastic
- Requires more frequent watering, especially in summer

Plastic

Advantages

- Inexpensive
- Lightweight
- Wide variety of shapes, sizes, and colors
- Excellent for propagating and short-term growing
- Needs less watering in dry conditions

Disadvantages

- Holds moisture, increasing susceptibility to wet soil and root rot
- Requires accurate watering
- Not adaptable to high humidity because soil stays moister longer; plants can't transpire freely

Wood (tubs, half-barrels)

Advantages

- Good for big plants
- Variety of choices (redwood, cypress, cedar)
- Decorative and earthy

Disadvantages

- Limited wicking advantage
- Decays with time
- Heavy to lift, especially when waterlogged

Cement

Advantages

- Many forms available
- Available in large, monumental sizes
- Long-lasting
- Good focal points
- Sturdy in high-wind areas

Disadvantages

- Cannot winter over outside unless emptied and inverted
- Heavy to lift and move
- Nonporous, with no wicking action
- Often lack drainage hole
- Can be expensive

Glazed Ceramic

Advantages

- Many decorative designs and sizes
- Available in a wide price range
- Attractive for use as jardinières

Disadvantages

- Limited moisture and air flow through container due to glazing
- Often lack drainage hole
- Breakable

continued from page 126

Potting mixes sold at nurseries and garden centers are a blend of sphagnum peat moss, composted pine bark, perlite, and vermiculite. Some mixes contain rice hulls, coconut coir, or composted peanut hulls, all of which work well for container plants. The formulations vary. We have found that those with a higher percentage of bark and perlite create the best soil environment for most plants. Many potting mixes, especially peat-based mixes, contain some ground limestone. Limestone is added to provide a slightly acid pH, which is favorable for most plants. Many mixes also contain a small amount of synthetic fertilizer to give newly potted plants a boost.

Gardeners sometimes ask us whether they can use soil dug from their garden to fill their containers rather than buying a potting mix. We don't ever recommend this. Garden soil compacts easily when put in containers, which means plant roots won't be able to expand easily or get enough air. Also, garden soil may contain harmful microorganisms as well as plant pests.

Adding high-quality compost to potting mix, usually at 10 percent or less of the mix by volume, is beneficial. You can use commercial bagged compost or compost from your home compost pile. Be sure to screen homemade compost before adding it. Supplementing a potting mix with compost boosts the diversity of beneficial microorganisms in the mix, which will help combat root diseases.

We do not recommend mixes that contain water-retention pearls, because these mixes can hold water longer than is desirable, especially in cool weather and damp conditions. Also, we advise caution with mixes that contain a slow-release fertilizer, which consists of pearls of synthetic fertilizer that leach slowly into the mix, feeding the plants for months. If bags of such mix sit for a long time before being used, too much fertilizer can leach into the mix, and you could unintentionally overdose a newly potted plant. If you like slow-release fertilizers, a better bet is to add your own. (See Applying Fertilizer, page 131.) Check the label and buy potting mix that contains no slow-release form of fertilizer.

→ Repotting: Step by Step

1. Put some fresh potting mix in the bottom of the new, larger container. Use only enough to fill the container about one-eighth full. (There's no need to put any filler, such as stones or pieces of pottery, in the bottom for drainage.)

2. Tip the plant on its side and tap the root system out of its current pot.

3. Set the root system in place in the new container, centering the rootball and trunk. The top of the rootball should be about half an inch below the rim of the new pot. If necessary, remove the plant and add more mix until it sits at the right level.

4. Add more fresh potting mix to fill in around the rootball.

5. Tamp or pack down the mix so the plant is secure. You can do this by lifting the pot and tapping it on a hard surface several times.

6. Water the plant thoroughly.

Potting and Repotting

Whether a young potted plant has been started from a cutting, a graft, or seed, it will most likely be growing in a small container. But as plants grow, they need to form bigger root systems to support their enlarging branches and foliage, and eventually a crop of fruit. To allow this natural growth process to take place, you'll need to repot your plants into larger containers as they move toward maturity.

As a general rule of thumb, the size of the pot regulates the size of the plant. Plants that have filled out a container with roots will grow more slowly, and ultimately the size of the plant will be smaller. Conversely, plants that are given room for their root system to expand will grow larger. Thus, you can maintain some control of plant size by holding back or increasing the pot size.

It's best to increase pot size incrementally at each repotting. Choose a pot that is 2 to 4 inches bigger than the one the plant is currently growing in.

One key to success when repotting is to make sure the final soil line is half an inch below the rim of the pot. This allows water to collect when watering and

Dispelling a Myth

You may have read or heard that it's a good idea to trim the roots of a plant when you repot it. But we never cut the roots of our plants when we repot. We simply place them in the new pot, and they grow and acclimate to their new surroundings. Cutting the roots can put your plant under unnecessary stress.

prevents overflow. The old rootball should not be visible; even its top surface will be slightly covered by new mix.

You'll continue to repot your plants periodically as needed until the maximum pot size is reached. How often to repot varies depending on the type of plant, because plants grow at different rates. A banana may need repotting two or more times a year, while a miracle berry can grow well for years in the same pot.

What determines maximum pot size? It may be the type of plant that you're growing, or it may be the amount of growing space you have available. For example, avocados and chocolate plants won't reach mature fruiting stage until they're

growing in a pot that is 16 inches in diameter or larger. On the other hand, a miracle berry plant and some types of citrus can produce fruit well for years growing in an 8- to 10-inch pot.

Some plants with strong root systems respond well to repotting directly into a much larger pot (i.e., from a 4-inch pot to a 12-inch pot). However, it's wiser to step up the containers at a slower pace because of the risk for root disease. Root disease can develop when a small rootball sits in a large mass of surrounding soil because that soil can stay wet for long periods of time. Combine those wet soil conditions with cool temperatures, and it's very likely that roots will rot.

Maintaining Your Plants

Caring for plants from day to day is the real joy of gardening for many gardeners. It's the process more than the outcome of container gardening that provides satisfaction and reward, but with a little luck, you'll get to enjoy not only the pleasure of tending your plants, but a delicious harvest as well. Read on to learn our best tips and techniques for watering, fertilizing, and pruning or shaping container plants.

Watering

For container-grown plants, proper watering is the most important cultural practice. How you water your plants can make all the difference between success and failure. The physical act of watering is easy, but deciding *when* to water and *how much* to water requires some know-how.

Deciding When to Water

The best rule of thumb is to water your plant when the soil is visually dry. Most potting mixes are dark brown when they're saturated with moisture; they turn a light brown color when dry. You can also evaluate the plant's appearance. Is it visually in a wilt? If so, then water. An occasional slight wilt can be beneficial because it strengthens the plant by creating tougher tissue; it also indicates that the soil is quite dry, which means that pore space is open for air to infiltrate. Keep in mind, though, that at times a plant will wilt not because of lack of water but because of a poor root system or extreme heat. Avoid letting plants reach a state of severe wilt, because damage to foliage and leaf drop may result.

Another way to monitor moisture status is to touch the soil. If the soil surface feels damp to your fingers, no watering is needed. But if the surface is dry, poke your finger in below the soil surface. If you discover that the mix is still dry 1 inch below the surface, it's time to water. This method is especially helpful for hanging plants, for plants with foliage that grows tight to the soil surface, and for plants placed in bright sunlight where it's hard to tell visually whether the soil is wet or dry.

A third method is to simply lift the pot to see whether it is heavy or light. If it is light in weight, the plant likely needs watering.

How Much Water?

Once you've decided that it's time to water, the next question is how much water to give each plant. Using a watering can or other vessel, slowly add water at the soil surface until you see a small amount of water draining out at the bottom of the pot. This is enough to saturate the rootball. Then, wait until the soil is visually dry before watering again.

Fertilizers

Plants that are growing in soil in a garden can expand their roots out and down into new soil to find water and nutrients. When growing in a pot, however, a plant is dependent on the gardener, and it's the gardener's responsibility to "feed" the plant. Fertilizers are liquid or solid substances that supply the nutrients that plants need to thrive and grow roots, leaves, flowers, and fruit. Properly fertilizing and watering your plants helps to spur vigorous growth.

Garden centers offer a wide choice of fertilizers in bags and bottles. Some are synthetic, supplying nutrients in the form of chemical compounds referred to as "salts." Others are labeled as all-natural or organic; these are derived from plant, mineral, or animal sources. While the best synthetic formulations supply the same chemical nutrients as organic formulations, organic sources are usually a better source of micronutrients. Whatever type of fertilizer you decide to buy, read the product label to make sure it contains all the major and minor nutrients for plant growth. For starters, look for a series of three numbers, usually prominently listed on the front label. This is the NPK ratio, and it represents the percentage of nitrogen (N), phosphorus (P), and potassium (K) in the product. For example, 10–10–10 indicates that a product contains 10 percent nitrogen, 10 percent phosphorus (or more precisely, phosphate), and 10 percent potassium. The rest of the product is smaller amounts of other nutrients such as magnesium and iron, as well as inert ingredients.

Most plants do best with a balanced fertilizer, which is a product that has relatively equal NPK numbers. For instance, a 7–9–5 product is considered a balanced fertilizer, while a 10–5–5 product would be called a high-nitrogen fertilizer. (High-nitrogen formulas reduce or suppress flowering and fruit production.) A good-quality balanced fertilizer will also contain minor nutrients.

Organic Fertilizer

We recommend using organic fertilizers whenever possible, because they are generally less concentrated and so reduce the risk of overfertilization. Also, organic fertilizers are more sustainable for our environment. Fish emulsion, blood meal, and seaweed are prime examples of organic fertilizers, though it is usually best to buy a product that contains a mix of different nutrient sources. These materials contain the major nutrients that plants need plus myriad trace minerals. Occasionally, even organic fertilizer blends contain high levels of nitrates. Using these can result in a flush of leafy growth and not flowers. Choose one with a balanced formula (roughly equal NPK numbers) to avoid this problem.

Fish emulsion and seaweed fertilizer are two organic products that usually come in liquid form but can be very odiferous. That's fine for container plants outdoors on a deck or patio, but if you plan to use fish or seaweed fertilizer indoors, experiment first by fertilizing only one plant to see whether the smell bothers you.

Granular or powdered organic fertilizer products are generally not water-soluble and are used as a topdressing. These organic fertilizers actually work as slow-release fertilizers in a pot, and applications can be spread out over weeks if not months. Follow label directions for amounts and timing of a particular product.

Applying Fertilizer

You can feed your container plants in three different ways:

- Dissolve fertilizer in water and apply with each watering.
- Apply nonsoluble fertilizer granules or powder as a topdressing. Water into soil thoroughly.
- Mix in slow-release fertilizer beads at planting time, or apply to surface and gently mix into soil.

We get the best results by feeding our plants frequently with small amounts of balanced fertilizer. Your goal is to keep plants producing healthy growth while preventing a buildup of fertilizer salts that will harm plants. Keep in mind that some nutrients are washed out of a pot each time you water with plain water between feedings. And in areas with abundant rainfall, summer rains can leach out nutrients from containers placed outside on a deck or patio. This is actually better than having too much water and fertilizer accumulate

 Plant Nutrient Needs

Major Nutrients. The three most important major nutrients, also called macro-nutrients, are nitrogen, phosphorus, and potassium. Calcium, magnesium, and sulfur are also considered major plant nutrients, but they are not readily available in commercial fertilizers.

Minor Nutrients. The minor nutrients, also called micronutrients or trace minerals, are boron, chlorine, cobalt, copper, iron, manganese, molybdenum, nickel, and zinc.

in the mix, so we recommend not using drip catchers under containers. And if a container plant is set into a jardinière, you should dump out any liquid that accumulates in the jardinière after watering.

Applying smaller amounts of fertilizer more frequently works best because it constantly replenishes the supply of nutrients. A constant, low-level supply of fertilizer results in healthy, vigorous plants. The easiest way to achieve this is with liquid fertilizer or with a soluble fertilizer that is mixed with water.

Always follow application rates recommended on the label. More is not better! Never use *more* than the amounts recommended; you can often apply *less*. Any type of fertilizer applied in excess can lead to a buildup of fertilizer salts, and these salts can injure plant roots. Seaweed formulations in particular can lead to salt buildup if they are applied in excess. Some plants are more sensitive to salt injury than others. Be especially careful when fertilizing salt-sensitive plants. Also, if leaf edges of your plants start to turn brown, it may be due to excess fertilizer salts, and you may need to switch to a different type of fertilizer.

Slow-release fertilizers are a good choice if you don't want to have to keep track of when to fertilize. Most types consist of pearl-shaped beads that have a membrane that allows small amounts of fertilizer to leach out into moist soil over a period of 90 days or longer. You can apply the beads by top-dressing them evenly over the top of the rootball; they must be covered with soil in order to work. If you add them yourself at planting time and

mix in thoroughly, you avoid the risk of fertilizer burn that may occur with potting mixes that include premixed fertilizer. We don't recommend plant fertilizer sticks because the fertilizer concentrates in one area of the rootball, rather than being dispersed throughout the potting media.

If you place your plants outside during the summer in a spot where lots of rain will wash through the potting medium, you'll need to increase either the frequency or concentration of fertilizer, especially if foliage begins to turn pale yellow, which signals a lack of nutrients. This is easily corrected by doubling up for the next few feedings on the fertilizer quantity or frequency listed in the chart on page 133.

Light, Moderate, and Heavy Feeders

Some plants need more fertilizer than others. In the individual plant descriptions in this book, we classify plants as light feeders, moderate feeders, or heavy feeders.

Light feeders are sensitive to excess fertilizer. Typically they are slow growers cultured under low levels of light. When growth slows, stop fertilizing until longer days and warmer temperatures return.

Moderate feeders grow quickly under long day length and warmth. When growth slows, stop fertilizing until longer days and warmer temperatures return.

Heavy feeders are rapidly growing plants; if not fed heavily, their leaves will turn pale yellow and lower leaves will drop. Be prepared to be amazed at the amount of growth that will happen in one season.

The Perils of Overfeeding

- Lots of fertilizer will force quick growth, but often at the cost of the long-term health of the plant.
- Too much fertilizer produces soft, succulent leaves and stems that are more susceptible to attack by pests and pathogens.
- Excess fertilizer causes browning of leaf edges on sensitive plants.

Iron Deficiency

Also known as iron chlorosis, iron deficiency is one of the most common micronutrient problems in container-grown fruiting plants. It's easy to recognize: the leaf veins stay green while the rest of the leaf turns yellow. Iron chlorosis simply indicates that the plant is not absorbing enough iron. Either iron is not present in sufficient quantities in the potting mix, or a nutrient imbalance is preventing the roots from taking up the iron. The underlying problem is often a pH imbalance. Soil pH describes the alkalinity or acidity of soil and is measured on a scale of 1 to 14, with 7 as the neutral mark. A pH below 7 is considered acidic and pH above 7 is termed alkaline. Most plants prefer a slightly acidic range of 5.7 to 6.5; exceptions are noted in specific plant entries. Typically, you'll see chlorosis in

continued on page 134

Feeding Schedules for Container Plants

The chart below lists how much and how often to feed your plants based on whether they're light, moderate, or heavy feeders and whether you're using organic or soluble synthetic fertilizers. We've based these recommendations on an organic fertilizer with 5 percent available nitrogen (NPK ratio would start with a 5). The quantities for soluble synthetic fertilizers are based on a product with 15 percent available nitrogen. For optimum plant growth, we recommend applying smaller amounts of fertilizer more often.

With liquid fertilizer solutions, apply just enough fertilizer solution per plant to thoroughly saturate the potting medium. With granular fertilizers, for pots smaller or larger than 8 inches, decrease or increase the amount of fertilizer proportionately.

Remember to cut back on fertilizer as the days become shorter and plants slow their growth in the fall and winter. Also, it is important to reduce or stop fertilizing when the soil temperature drops below 60°F (15°C) on a consistent basis.

Plant Type	Fertilizer Type	Feeding Instructions
Light Feeders	Organic granular	1 tablespoon per 8-inch pot applied as a topdressing monthly
	Organic liquid	1 teaspoon per gallon of water; feed weekly. Or 1 tablespoon per gallon of water; feed monthly.
	Soluble synthetic	¼ teaspoon per gallon of water; feed weekly throughout the active growing season. Or 1 teaspoon per gallon of water; feed monthly.
Moderate Feeders	Organic granular	1½ tablespoons per 8-inch pot applied as a topdressing monthly
	Organic liquid	2 teaspoons per gallon of water; feed weekly. Or 1½ tablespoons per gallon of water; feed monthly.
	Soluble synthetic	½ teaspoon per gallon of water; feed weekly during the active growing season. Or 1 teaspoon per gallon of water; feed every other week, but apply clear water between feedings to prevent salt buildup.
Heavy Feeders	Organic granular	2 tablespoons per 8-inch pot applied as a topdressing monthly
	Organic liquid	1 tablespoon per gallon of water; feed weekly.
	Soluble synthetic	¼ teaspoon per gallon of water; use this solution every time you water. Or 1 teaspoon per gallon of water; feed once a week. Apply clear water at least twice a month to prevent salt buildup. In fall and winter, cut back to ¼–½ teaspoon per gallon of water applied weekly.

acid-loving plants that are growing in soil that is too alkaline.

It's easy to check the pH of the mix in a container using a simple pH test kit. If you discover that the pH is too alkaline, use one of the methods listed below to acidify the mix. If pH is not the problem, then the chlorosis may be due to cool root temperatures or root disease, both of which can prevent the absorption of iron.

If you see iron chlorosis, first check the plant's root system for root disease by tipping the rootball out of the container and inspecting it. Are the roots white and succulent or brown and dead? Pull gently on the roots to see if they are viable (for more details, see Root Disease on page 149). If the roots are healthy, immediately move the plant into warmer conditions and give it an iron tonic. Use a special, readily absorbable type of iron called chelated iron. Simply dilute in water following the

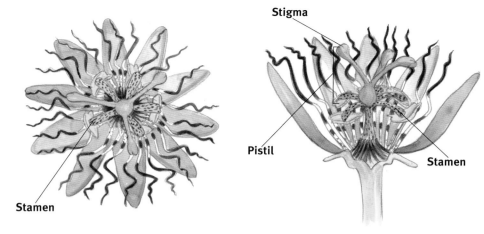

These passionflowers provide a dramatic example of flower structure. To hand-pollinate any flower, first identify the stamen, which bears the pollen, and the pistil, which is the female structure. Transfer pollen from the stamen to the stigma (the tip of the pistil).

label instructions and then splash or mist the leaves and water the plant's soil with the solution. Repeat applications at weekly intervals until the problem is solved.

Pollinating Plants by Hand

In their native habitat, most fruiting plants are pollinated by insects. Some are pollinated by birds or other wildlife, or simply by the wind. But when you grow plants in containers, you can't always rely on insects, animals, or even sufficient wind being present to do a thorough job of pollination. Fortunately, it's easy to hand-pollinate flowers to ensure good fruit set.

You can simply brush your hand across the pistils and stamens of a flower. This method works well for pollinating dragon fruit; it must be done in the evening once the flower is fully open. To pollinate miracle berry, just rustle the branches on sunny, warm days.

With large flowers such as those on passion fruit, you can pick a pollen pad (anther) off the flower of the pollen-bearing plant and rub it onto the pistil of the fruiting plant. Chocolate trees also benefit from this kind of hand-pollinating.

A third technique is to use a small artist's paintbrush to swipe pollen off an anther and dab it onto the pistil. It's best to do this when the flower is fully open. This technique works well for pollinating sapodilla flowers.

Pruning

We can't stress enough the importance of pruning. It can be an exciting and liberating process. As a gardener, you get to create a plant that is just right for you and your growing space. Trimming, shaping, and pruning to maintain height in a manageable and aesthetically pleasing form is your goal. In the long run, pruning is the

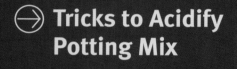

Tricks to Acidify Potting Mix

- Top-dress with cottonseed meal; sprinkle meal on the soil surface and water well.

- Switch to an acidifying fertilizer that contains ammonium sulfate (such fertilizers are not organic). Or use an organic product designed for rhododendrons and camellias.

- Make a dilute solution of black tea, and water the plant every week or two with the solution.

only way to create a full and productive plant that will fit in the space you have available. A vigorous plant such as acerola needs to be trimmed back on a regular basis or it will outgrow its container. Others such as miracle berry are slow growers that need only an occasional trim.

As with children, giving a plant the appropriate environment to grow in will help to shape it for the future. Make decisions about placement, form, and shape of your fruiting container plant when your plant is young. Learn the plant's growth habit so you can plan accordingly (you can find information on growth habit in the plant entries). Some plants, such as coffee, naturally grow best with a central leader form and thus need little in the way of an initial pruning. Others, such as a banana tree, are pruned back only after flowering and fruiting is complete.

When growing plants that produce fruit, pruning well becomes even more important, because how and when you prune can affect flowering and fruiting. Timing is critical. The optimal time to prune many fruiting plants is after harvest; otherwise you could inadvertently do in the next crop by cutting off the new flower buds. You'll find specific recommendations on when and how to prune in the individual plant entries throughout this book.

If you mistakenly prune a plant at the wrong time of year, patience is called for. Eventually the plant will regrow, resume flowering, and bear another crop of fruit. On rare occasions, though, even a normally vigorous plant may fail to come back after hard pruning. In our experience, this is due not to the shock of removing

⊕ Plant Forms

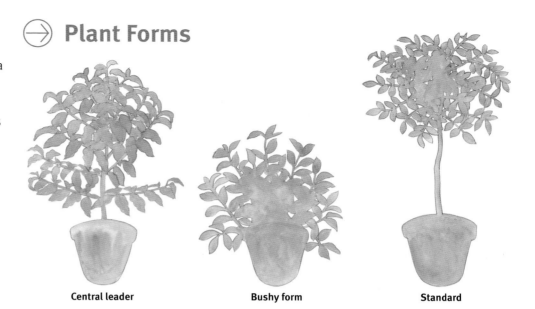

Central leader   Bushy form   Standard

You can train a fruiting container plant to one of three basic forms: an upright plant with a central leader; a bushy shrub or small tree; or an informal or formal standard.

the foliage alone. Rather, the plant was already predisposed to failure because of a poor root system. So if one of your plants dies after you prune it, check the roots before you take the blame.

Shaping Young Plants

Some gardeners cringe at the thought of cutting back young plants, but the sacrifice of immediate growth and fruit will result in a better plant specimen in the long run. Citrus plants such as 'Ponderosa' lemon are a prime example. Pruning to promote sturdy stems must begin when these plants are young, because individual fruits can weigh 5 pounds or more. Without a solid framework, the plants won't be able to support the heavy fruit.

Training is important in establishing plant shape, but plant shape also

⊕ Pinching a Young Plant

Removing the growing tip by pinching it off with your fingers or a pruning tool stimulates the development of side shoots.

Before pinching   New growth after pinching

Plants That (Almost) Never Need Pruning

- Banana (page 58)
- Miracle berry (page 74)
- Pineapple (page 92)
- Vanilla (page 122)

 ### Plants That Need Hard Pruning

- Avocado (page 56)
- Citrus (all types)
- Fig (page 66)
- June plum (page 72)
- Orangeberry (page 82)
- Peanut butter fruit (page 90)
- Tree tomato (page 102)
- Yerba maté (page 112)

depends on whether or not a plant was grown from a seedling or cutting or was grafted onto a rootstock. Seedling-grown specimens of plants such as guava or noni often have more upright vigor. Cutting-grown plants tend more to a multi-stemmed habit, especially when young. Growing conditions such as fertilizer and light level also affect the shape of a plant.

Consider the following factors as you decide what shape would work best for a new plant that you're adding to your collection:

- Growing space: Will it be an indoor plant, an outdoor plant, or will you move it from indoors to out depending on the season?

- Pot size: Do you have a limited amount of space and thus need to keep the plant contained in a small pot, or can you let the plant grow large and full?

- Growth habit: Does the plant have potential to develop with a full, bushy, dense form? Does it have a strong central stem, which would allow you to train it as a standard? Or is it a climber?

Training a standard can be fun. Plants that have a natural upright central stemmed habit or a branching growth habit can be trained as a standard. (See page 138.) A coffee plant has a natural central leader and most citrus plants can be used for standards by training the dominant stem as a central lead.

If you prefer a more informal look, you can allow upright growers such as figs to branch out into full, bushy specimens. To encourage branching, it is important to "pinch" the growing tip when the plant is a young cutting or seedling. New shoots will then sprout from the buds lower down the main stem, resulting in a multi-stemmed plant. We recommend training citrus as multiple-stemmed specimens as well so they can hold an abundance of fruit. You can use your fingers to literally pinch off the soft tip growth. When a plant stems get older and thicker, a tool such as pruning shears is needed to accomplish this task.

With a young plant, wait until the plant is 6–8 inches tall to pinch it. Check to make sure there are four or five axillary buds along the stem (these buds are located at the base of each leaf stem).

Pruning Mature Plants

A plant is considered mature once it has gone through a flowering and fruiting cycle. Size is not the determining factor for maturity of container plants. Pot size puts a limit on growth, and thus a plant can reach maturity even when it's relatively small.

In general, when you prune a plant, make a clean cut just above a leaf; be sure to leave the bud that sits just above the base of the leaf stem (the axillary bud) intact, as shown below. Cutting back a stem changes the balance of certain plant

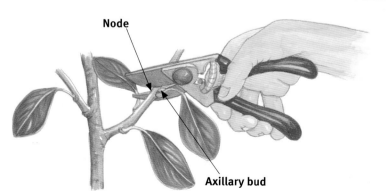

Node

Axillary bud

When making a pruning cut, position your pruners on an angle just above the node. Avoid cutting into the axillary bud.

hormones, which stimulates a new shoot to grow from this lateral bud.

A heading cut, also called heading back, is removal of part of a branch. Heading cuts promote remaining buds to sprout into lateral branches and thus lead to a fuller, bushy look. Cutting a branch back all the way to the plant's main stem is called a thinning cut. Thinning cuts don't stimulate regrowth the way that heading cuts do. They result in a more open plant form.

There is no single rule of thumb for how much and how often to prune mature plants. Some mature plants hardly ever need pruning. Others will need a periodic or seasonal pruning to limit plant size for your container or growing area. Sometimes you'll need to prune to restructure a plant. For example, if left to its own, a citrus plant can become open and scraggly. In that case, you'll need to head back overly long branches to allow new shoots to fill in closer to the main stems, thus creating a full and more symmetrical specimen.

Fast-growing plants like the tree tomato need a hard annual pruning, from which they resprout with ease. Hard or severe pruning is cutting back the plant close to the same size it was when you pruned it the last time around. When we prune a plant severely, we remove two-thirds of the plant's growth, using a combination of heading and thinning cuts. This harsh treatment disrupts flowering but is necessary to maintain size and form. We are always amazed to see how quickly vigorous plants rebound with flowering and fruiting after drastic pruning.

 # Pruning: Heading Cuts and Thinning Cuts

Pruning mature plants is done by making heading cuts, thinning cuts, or a combination of both. A heading cut shortens a shoot or branch, while a thinning cut removes the shoot or branch entirely.

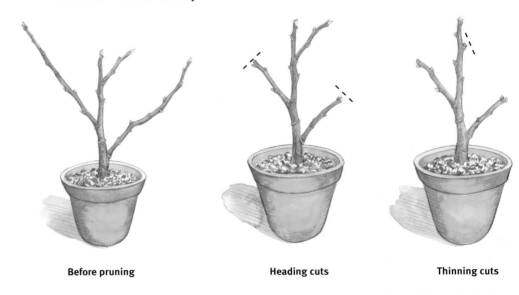

| Before pruning | Heading cuts | Thinning cuts |

Selective pruning is different from hard pruning. In general, selective pruning is best for slow-growing plants such as guava. In this case, you cut back branches to control overall size, but you don't remove wood on which new flower buds or new fruits have already set. (The flowers and fruit usually form on the flush of new growth.) Once you see fruit beginning to form, any branches that have gotten out of hand can be trimmed back to just above the set fruit. This allows fruit that has already set to mature while keeping the general form of the plant intact. Selective pruning can be done once or twice a season. Guava, citrus fruits, Australian beach cherry, and olive are examples of plants that respond well to selective pruning.

Best Time to Prune

With container plants, unless you have unlimited space, you'll always have to sacrifice some fruit in order to keep the plant from outgrowing its space. The best time to prune is generally right after a flowering cycle, when fruit is newly set. This allows you to decide the balance between how much fruit you want to leave on your plant and how much growth you want to prune off to keep the specimen contained. Since some branches will have set more fruit than others, you can choose to leave the more productive branches untouched and prune off the branches that have less fruit on them.

Another good time to prune is just as plants are beginning to grow in late winter or at a time when they are just breaking dormancy. Figs, for example, flower and set fruit on new growth. If you prune to shape or contain the form of the plant just as it breaks dormancy, then you won't interrupt the flowering and fruiting cycle. Peanut butter fruit, guava, and orange-berry also respond well to pruning before new growth starts.

During the long days of summer or the short days of winter, plants can be pruned again, depending on their fruiting cycle. Acerola, Australian beach cherry, and guava can be pruned in either summer or winter to maintain size and form. Citrus, however, has its heaviest fruit set in spring, so the best time to prune citrus is just after the spring crop of fruit sets. Selective pruning in the spring leaves some fruit on the plant, which then has the entire summer to mature. The next flush of growth will occur in late winter and produce the new flowers for the next crop of fruit.

Training a Standard

A standard is an upright plant that is trained to have a bare central trunk and a crown of growth on top. Training a standard is unique, exciting, and challenging. Culturing a plant as a treelike standard brings a formal grace and beauty into any garden space. Guava, citrus fruits, and June plum are good examples of fruiting plants that will adapt to this form. A few plants, such as papaya, form standards naturally.

 Steps in Training a Standard

1. Select a young plant that has a natural central leader or a dominant branch that can be trained as the main stem of the standard. (Seed-grown plants tend to have central leaders; cutting-grown plants often are multi-branched.)

2. Cut back all other branches flush with the central leader.

3. Repot the plant in a larger container to allow for the expanding root system. Usually this means a pot 2–4 inches larger than the current container.

4. Allow the plant to grow taller. As it grows, cut off all vigorous offshoots or side branches that form, but do not remove individual leaves that sprout directly from the main stem. These leaves will provide energy for the plant to help hasten overall growth of the plant.

5. Prune off the tip of the central leader once it has reached the desired height. This will force buds below the cut to initiate growth, creating multiple new side stems and the beginning of a crown.

6. Once the top lateral buds have sprouted and formed shoots with two or three sets of leaves, pinch the growing tip of each shoot to cause it to branch. If your goal is a dense, thickly stemmed crown, then pinch each shoot one more time after the next flush of new growth.

For a plant to grow well as a standard, it should have the following characteristics:

- Upright growth habit with short internodes (spaces between the leaf stems along a branch)
- Fast growth (optional)
- Freely branching habit (each pruned stem will produce two or more side shoots)

A standard may take anywhere from six months to two years to create. The taller you want your standard to be, the longer it will take. Large-fruited plants need to be trained as tall standards in order to hold the mature crown of growth (for guava, for example, the bare central stem should at least be 3–4 feet). Follow the steps above to train your fruiting container plant as a standard.

Once your standard has reached the desired size and started to produce fruit, you'll need to prune it occasionally to maintain general form. Be sure to remove any suckers that sprout at the base or along the trunk. Also cut back any branches that are out of proportion to the crown overall.

Severe pruning may be necessary to contain the size and maintain the form. Severe pruning is usually done after fruiting and may delay the next cycle of flowers and fruit. For guavas, prune stems back to the point of the initial final pinch (see step 6 at left).

Training Vines and Climbers

Black pepper, vanilla, and passion fruit stems all grow too long for a small pot on a windowsill. They do well when trained to grow on a stake, trellis, or hoop. You can use plant ties to encourage the vines to climb their support.

Black pepper and passion fruit vines can be grown in hanging baskets, too. Direct the stems around the rim of the pot and allow them to hang over the edge, trailing down with flowers and fruit. Any time the vines become too long, redirect them up and around the pot again.

At some point, vining plants can overwhelm the container and support they are growing on, especially passion fruit. The older stems often lose their leaves and the plants can start to look ragged. To remedy this, once the fruit is harvested, prune the plant hard; the bare stems will resprout.

Slow-growing black pepper and vanilla can be left unpruned for many years. When grown in a pot, vanilla needs as much vine as possible to encourage flowering.

Propagation

You can propagate some fruiting plants, such as miracle berry and orangeberry, by sowing the seeds and raising the seedlings to maturity. It's also interesting and fun to try out other propagation methods such as taking cuttings, air layering, and grafting.

New Plants from Cuttings

If you grow houseplants, you've undoubtedly tried rooting trimmed stems by sticking them in a small container of water. Many foliage houseplants will take root easily with this simple technique. To root cuttings from fruiting plants, though, it's advisable to use a rooting medium rather than plain water. The basic process is simple. You take the cuttings, dip the cut ends in rooting hormone, and stick the cut ends into a shallow container of moist rooting medium. Sand is an excellent medium, as is perlite. Commercial rooting media (such as Oasis) also work well but are expensive and can dry out readily. A standard sterile soilless mix can be used for rooting tree tomato, passion fruit, and 'Ponderosa' lemon.

How to Take a Cutting

There are two types of cuttings: tip cuttings and stem cuttings. A tip cutting will often grow to be a symmetrical and mature-looking young plant. This is a good choice if you want to create a standard. One problem with tip cuttings is the mother plant's new leaves may be too "soft" to root easily. If this is the case, you'll need to watch the plant as it grows and take cuttings when the terminal leaves are mature and firm. Some plants grow so quickly that they seldom have mature leaves. If this is the case, then take stem cuttings from fully mature stems rather than tip cuttings. Also, stem cuttings are the best choice when quantity is your goal. You can generate lots of stem cuttings from a single stock plant.

Tip cuttings. Use a knife or pruning shears to cut off the topmost part of a stem, including the growing tip. Strip off all but the top two or three mature leaves.

Stem cuttings. Cut off a length of stem and remove the top few inches, including the terminal bud. Cut the remaining length of stem into segments that are 3–6 inches long with several leaves per segment. Strip off the lower leaf on each segment. If a cutting has very large leaves, cut each individual leaf in half to reduce the total surface area of foliage. This will prevent

→ Rooting a Cutting

To root a cutting, you can position a node along the cut stem below the surface of the rooting mix (left), and roots will sprout at the node. Or you can dip a cut stem in rooting hormone and leave the lowest stem node above soil level (right). The hormone will promote root formation.

Node above potting soil

Node below potting soil

the plant from losing too much moisture through transpiration.

Dip the end of each cutting into root gel, liquid hormone, or rooting powder. Poke holes in the rooting medium with a pencil or chopstick, and insert the treated ends of the cuttings into the holes. Then water thoroughly to settle the medium, which will help to hold the cuttings in place.

The challenge with cuttings is to keep them from drying out during the period when they are forming roots. Once a cutting has formed callus (thick, protective tissue) on the cut surface, it can take up moisture more easily. Enclose rooted cuttings in a clear plastic bag; this will help maintain high levels of humidity. Keep cuttings out of the direct sunlight of midday. Exposure to early morning sun or late afternoon sun is okay. Maintain temperatures at 70–75°F (21–23°C) for optimum rooting. Cooler temperatures will slow down the rooting process.

Air Layering

Air layering is the process of rooting a stem while it is still attached to its mother plant. This technique is useful for propagating plants that won't root well by conventional cuttings, such as Australian beach cherry, chocolate plant, and cinnamon. It's a time-consuming process, but it is a surefire way of generating a new plant. Here's how:

1. Select a mature branch at least 6–8 inches long.

2. Make a wound by girdling the stem 8–16 inches back from the tip. Generally, mature wood with enough stem is ideal. To do this, use a pocketknife to make a cut through the bark and peel off a layer all the way around the stem. Also scrape away the cambium layer (bark) of the exposed area until the wood of the stem is fully exposed.

3. Apply rooting hormone to the wound.

4. Soak a handful of sphagnum moss in water until saturated. Cover the area around the wound with a clump of the saturated moss. Wrap plastic food wrap or

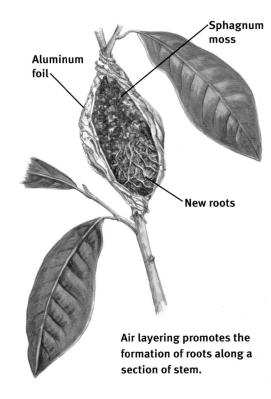

Air layering promotes the formation of roots along a section of stem.

aluminum foil or both around the moss. You can secure the plastic or foil in place simply by twisting it at each end, creating a seal around the sphagnum moss. Make sure there is no moss poking out or else moisture will be wicked away.

5. Check the moss periodically by opening up the wrap a bit and feeling for moisture in the moss. Add water with a watering can as needed to keep moss moist. After several weeks, start checking for roots. It can take from several weeks to months for roots to grow in the moist moss.

6. Once roots have expanded into the moss, use pruners to cut just below the rooted portion to remove the air-layered stem from the plant.

Gel, Powder, or Liquid?

We use root hormone gel on plants that are more difficult to root because it tends to stick to the plant tissue better than liquid or powdered hormone products. Powdered hormones are readily available and inexpensive, and they are a better choice for plants such as papaya, for which the concentrated liquids and gels are too strong.

7. Pot up the rooted stem in a container filled with potting mix. It is important to provide high humidity until the root system has established itself in the mix and the plant can take up enough water to reduce stress.

8. If the rooted cutting goes into a severe wilt, place the container, cutting and all, inside a plastic bag and seal it closed. Or trim back the leaves to reduce moisture loss due to transpiration.

Grafting

Grafting is the process by which a cut stem of one plant, referred to as a scion, is united with the stem base and roots, called a rootstock or understock, of another plant. A scion and understock generally must belong to the same genus or family; otherwise, the graft won't be successful.

Grafting is done to impart more vigor or disease resistance to a particular species or cultivar, or to propagate plants that won't root on their own. Grafting is a common way to propagate many types of fruiting plants, both tropical and temperate.

Cleft grafting is the easiest technique to master. The top growth of the understock is cut off and a vertical split is made in the exposed stem surface. The cut end of the scion piece is then shaped into a wedge and slid into the split in the understock stem. The scion and understock must be the same diameter in order to allow their circulatory tissue (cambium) to accurately make contact and grow together. The point of union is secured with a rubber band, grafting tape, or other material. Leaves are usually removed from the scion, and the scion can be wrapped in grafting tape as well to prevent it from desiccating. For some plants, a humidity tent of plastic or a glass jar is placed over the graft to keep it from drying out before the union connects. For deciduous plants a humidity tent is not needed, because the stems for the scions are cut when the plant is dormant (leafless).

Pests and Diseases

Plant pests and diseases are part of the natural balance in outdoor gardens, but even with container plants, it's inevitable that some pest and disease problems will crop up. Your goal as a gardener is to keep your plants flourishing despite an occasional outbreak.

One approach to dealing with pests and disease is to rid the plant of the problem by using chemicals that kill the pest or pathogen. This is old thinking, and although it will eradicate pests temporarily, there are serious consequences to the environment and human health. We prefer to work on a more integrated level, monitoring our plants frequently for pest and disease problems and taking steps to manage them through cultural and biological controls or environmentally safe pesticides. This approach has moved into the mainstream of horticulture as sustainability for our planet becomes more imperative.

We love using predatory insects to control pests in greenhouses and in the home environment. Releasing natural predators of spider mites and aphids in particular is the simplest way to control these pests. And relying on beneficial insects rather than spraying individual plants can be a real time-saver if you have a large collection of container plants. It's important to refrain from using insecticides while beneficial insects are present. If insecticides have been used in the past, give your plants a waiting period of several weeks for the residual chemicals to clear before releasing insect predators. A general rule of thumb for using beneficial insects is to release the predator when pest populations are low. Several releases are usually needed to ensure control of the pests.

The last option for pest and disease control is to do nothing and let nature take its course. This can work at times but often at the expense of the plants and the fruit that you want to harvest.

Whatever treatment philosophy you decide to adopt, your first task is always to identify the pest or disease, understand its habits, and then gain control through treatment.

Eight Container Plant Pests

Container plant pests fall into two basic categories: mobile and less mobile. Mobile insects crawl or fly; they include aphids, spider mites, whiteflies, and thrips. You may notice a sudden flush of these pests when you bring plants inside from their summer growing space. The pests took up residence during the summer, but not until they are brought inside away from natural predators do the populations increase and become noticeable.

The less-mobile pests are mainly mealybugs, scale, and occasionally slugs and snails. Although they do not fly, these pests can still be transferred from one plant to another. (See How Pests Get Onto Your Plants on page 145.)

Aphids

Description

Aphids, also known as plant lice, are soft-bodied insects that usually feed on soft growth. The adult stage has wings. Because aphids can reproduce asexually, their populations can expand very quickly.

Telltale Signs

Look for aphids near the buds and growing tips, as well as black sooty mold on leaf surfaces. The mold grows on sugars that the aphids excrete as they feed.

Another sign is white flecks or chaffing on the leaves, which are simply the old skins of the molting insects. When this is seen, look closely for small green, black, or reddish insects.

Treatment

Sometimes a valid approach for treatment is to do nothing. If it's springtime, once you move your container plants outside, the aphids may disappear thanks to naturally occurring lacewings and other predators that move onto the plants on their own. Wait and see if the natural balance can be achieved. If an infestation crops up indoors in fall or winter, though, some remedial procedure is needed.

For large plant rooms and greenhouses, we highly recommend the use of beneficial or predatory insects to control aphids. Buying and releasing beneficials may seem expensive, but in our experience, the ease of control they provide is worth every penny. We have used purchased beneficial insects at home and in the greenhouses at Logee's. It's easy to do. Order the appropriate predator from a supplier (see the resources on page 155 for listings). Simply open the jar of insects, sprinkle them on the infested plants, and wait. There are several excellent predatory or beneficial insects for controlling aphids (see Best Beneficials for Aphid Control below). For small collections, lacewing larvae are best. In our large greenhouses at Logee's we have resident populations of *Aphidius* wasps and *Aphidoletes* midges, and we work to encourage their presence by raising "banker plants." That is, we grow specific varieties of plants that are highly prone to aphids and allow the predators to regenerate on these plants. Or if aphid colonies arise on any of our stock plants, we set them aside as banker plants, too. We stop taking cuttings from them but leave them, in the greenhouse as a home for our predatory insects. In return, our predators clean up the pesky aphids.

A spray of plain water can be used to reduce aphid populations, but it is hard to achieve complete control this way. If even one aphid is left on a plant, then the population will quickly rebound. We don't like to use insecticidal soaps because of the risk that they will damage plant foliage, especially if repeated applications are used. And, to gain control, more than one spraying is needed of most insecticides, whether chemical or organic.

Spider Mites

Description

Spider mites are tiny, slow-moving creatures related to spiders. The most common spider mite found on container plants is the two-spotted spider mite. Some types of plants are more prone to spider mite problems than others. Spider mites tend to proliferate under hot, dry conditions like those found indoors in the winter or in the high heat of summer. They are suppressed by cool, damp conditions.

 # Best Beneficials for Aphid Control

Aphidius colemani

This tiny wasp lays its eggs inside the bodies of aphids. The wasp larvae literally eat the aphid and then pupate inside the hollow body, which looks like a bit of brown puff. Once you see these brown puffs appearing in an aphid colony, that infestation is finished. It may take a week or longer, but the aphids will eventually be overwhelmed.

Aphidoletes

Also called the gall midge, this tiny flea-like insect lays its eggs among a colony of aphids. The larvae pierce the aphid bodies and suck out the fluids. Gall midges are very effective at decimating aphid infestations. The larvae, once mature, fall to the soil to pupate. Adults will re-emerge to start another generation.

Lacewings

These beneficials are good for spot treatment of infested plants. Most suppliers offer the larval stage of this insect, which you can place directly on the leaves of plants that are infested with aphids.

How Pests Get onto Your Plants

Sometimes pests seem to spontaneously appear on a container plant indoors, and you may wonder how on earth they got there. Here are three possible solutions to the mystery:

1. If you buy a plant or receive one as a gift, it may already have pests lurking on the leaf undersides or in the soil mix.

2. A plant that is pest-free may be an attractive target to pests that are hanging out on nearby plants. Even nonflying pests such as mealybugs can crawl from one container plant to another, or you may inadvertently transfer them on tools or your hands as you work among your plants.

3. Some pests and disease pathogens are highly mobile and may be blown long distances on the wind or in water droplets. They may land on your plants during the summer when the plants are outdoors on a deck or patio, but you may not notice the pest or disease symptoms until you've brought the plants back indoors.

to bring a spider mite outbreak under control, but it can remain alive in a grouping of plants even when no spider mites are present because it can also feed on pollen and other types of mites.

To ensure good results, release the predatory mites at the first sign of spider mites. Once released, the predators will move from plant to plant searching for prey. As long as the leaves of adjacent plants are touching, the mites will disperse and consume all of the spider mites. In the North, spider mite problems often appear a month or two after plants are brought indoors for the winter. If you live in the North, release predatory mites even before signs of an infestation become visible, especially if you are growing plants that tend to be susceptible to spider mites.

Telltale Signs

Tiny, light-colored pinpricks on the leaf surface, usually in a grouping, are signs of spider mites. Turn the leaf over and check the underside with a magnifier. Usually a 10x or stronger will show the presence of tiny mites. As populations grow, plant webbing will appear. When it does, the problem needs to be addressed quickly or the plant will lose its leaves.

Treatment

The easiest way to get rid of spider mites is to spray cold water on the plant. It's important to spray all surfaces, especially the undersides of leaves. Take the infested plants outside and use a garden hose. Inside, you can put small plants in your kitchen sink and use the spray faucet; put larger plants in the shower.

Re-spray every day or two for a week, the more often the better. This treatment dislodges the adults, nymphs, and eggs while raising the humidity and cooling down the leaf surface, which will eventually cause the population to crash.

Neem oil products also work well for controlling mites; see Fighting Pests with Neem Oil on page 146.

Purchasing and releasing predatory mites that eat spider mites is extremely effective for large home collections and sunroom or greenhouse environments. Ask a biocontrols supplier for *Phytoseiulus persimilis* mites or *Amblyseius* (also sold as *Neoseiulus) californicus* mites. (See the resources on page 155.) Both work well on fruiting container plants. The former, a very aggressive predator, is the one that we most often use. The latter takes longer

Whiteflies

Description

Whiteflies are small white insects that fly off the plant when disturbed.

Telltale Signs

The most visible sign of a whitefly problem other than the adult flies is small scar-like bumps on leaf undersides. These are the immature stage of the insect and are called instars. Symptoms may also include formation of a black sooty mold on the leaves. The life cycle from egg to adult is usually one month under normal temperatures; all life stages can be found together on leaf undersides. Controls are designed to intercept one or all of these stages. Tree tomato and naranjilla are especially susceptible to whitefly.

Treatment

Neem oil is an effective treatment for whiteflies. It smothers eggs and adults and interferes with one instar stage. See Fighting Pests with Neem Oil, below, for application instructions. Usually three applications, applied one week apart, are needed to ensure that the whitefly life cycle is broken.

Some predatory insects are effective against whitefly, but it takes time to see results. Low levels of whitefly will be present while the predators do their job. *Encarsia formosa* and *Eretmocerus eremicus* are two species of tiny wasps that parasitize whitefly pupae. Temperatures must be 60°F (15°C) or higher to stimulate the predators to reproduce quickly enough to keep up with the whiteflies.

This beneficial insect is helpful for low- to medium-density whitefly populations.

Delphastus catalinae is a small lady beetle that wanders over infected plants seeking out whiteflies (and spider mites too) and literally sucks all the life out of them.

In sunrooms and conservatories where whitefly populations are extensive, it is best to reduce those populations by applying a neem product before releasing the beneficial insects.

Thrips

Description

Thrips are very small insects that have long, thin bodies. They are often hard to spot on plants. Thrips are highly mobile insects that fly and are blown long distances by air currents.

Telltale Signs

The symptoms of thrip infestation are pitting or spotting on the leaves. Thrip damage on flowers usually appears on the edges of the blooms; flowers can become discolored and may have dried edges. Damage appears similar to spider mite damage, but thrip markings are larger and more streaking occurs. Western flower thrips, the most common species that container gardeners confront, feed on flowers and young leaves, and the damage becomes evident only as the leaves mature. Thrips are difficult to control because part of their life cycle takes place on leaves but they pupate in soil. The good news is that thrips prefer certain plants, such as blue- and purple-flowered plants in the African violet family. Thrips will attack the young foliage of citrus but avoid most tropical fruiting plants. When plants are placed outdoors, natural predators usually give good control.

Treatment

Neem oil will smother thrip eggs, nymphs, and adults. Repeated application is needed to ensure effectiveness: polish leaves weekly for four weeks. (See Fighting Pests with Neem Oil at left for application instructions.)

Spinosad, a biological pesticide, is effective against thrips. Apply it for several weeks according to the label directions to break the life cycle. Keep in mind that spinosad does have some toxicity to other beneficial insects, so spray only thrip-infested plants.

⊕ Fighting Pests with Neem Oil

Neem oil comes from the neem tree, and it can be used to treat a wide range of insect pests and diseases. We prefer products that are pure neem oil, which smothers mite eggs and adults and kills or deters several types of insect pests. This product is sold as a leaf polisher, so when you are polishing your leaves you fight pest problems too. Dilute 2 tablespoons of pure neem oil in 1 gallon of water and add 1½ teaspoons of dish detergent (which helps to emulsify or spread the oil). Usually you will need to spray this polish on the leaves twice,

four to five days apart if temperatures are 75°F (23°C) or higher, or weekly if temperatures are cooler.

Caution: When using neem oil to fight pests on indoor plants, wash the foliage with clear water to remove the oil before you repeat the application process for a third or subsequent time. Otherwise, oil may build up on the leaves and result in foliar damage, especially in high heat conditions. When plants are outdoors, rainfall usually prevents oil buildup.

→ Quarantine Plants to Prevent Problems

Mealybugs and other not-so-mobile pests are generally introduced into a collection of existing plants from a newly introduced plant. Because of this, whenever you bring home a new plant from the garden center or receive one by mail order or as a gift, keep it isolated until you're sure it is free of pest problems. Four to six weeks is a good length of time to keep a new plant in quarantine. Also, if you have an infested plant, be sure you wash your hands and tools after you prune, harvest, or care for the plant in any way. Otherwise, you may inadvertently carry mealybugs and scale insects to your healthy plants on your hands, tools, or watering can.

A tiny beetlelike insect called the minute pirate bug (*Orius insidiosus*) will prey on thrips from about March through October. This aggressive predator feeds on a wide variety of small soft-bodied insects. To get control, the release rate needs to be high: one bug for every 1½ square feet of growing area. The release rate that's worked best in our greenhouses is once every two weeks for six weeks.

Remember that plants have to be untouched by chemical pesticides for several weeks before the release of beneficials or else the residual chemicals may harm them.

Mealybugs

Description

Mealybugs are small white pests that are protected during most of their life cycle by a cottony mass or a waxy covering on the surface of their bodies. This protection makes them particularly difficult to eradicate. Mealybugs are primarily a pest of potted citrus. It's no coincidence that the most common species found on fruiting plants is the citrus mealybug.

Telltale Signs

A white cottony mass appears at the base of leaf stems or on leaf undersides. A black sooty mold may also appear on leaves. Egg masses are embedded in the cottony material. When the eggs hatch, tiny "crawlers" move out onto the leaf surface and may be observed moving slowly on leaf undersides. This stage is vulnerable to sprays and other control measures. As the insects mature, they develop a waxy coating that repels water and pesticides. Populations multiply very quickly in hot environments.

Treatment

Control is difficult because eggs and crawlers can remain inside the cottony masses for weeks and even months at a time. The adults will also tuck egg masses into crevices and curled-up leaves or behind plant ties, making it very difficult to coat the eggs with a spray. The good news is that as long as plants aren't touching, mealybugs cannot move from one plant to a nearby plant. Thus, the best approach is to isolate infested plants and work over time to rid them of mealybugs.

Mealybug is one of the few insects for which we still use a synthetic pesticide, an insect growth regulator called buprofezin, which disrupts the life cycle of the mealybug rather than killing it. Three applications are needed a week apart. Buprofezin has low mammalian toxicity and is harmless to beneficials, but we still don't recommend spraying when your plant is fruiting.

Neem oil will smother crawlers and eggs. The trick is to polish on a regular basis until control is achieved; see Fighting Pests with Neem Oil on page 146. A cedar oil product such as Ced-O-Flora can also be used to control mealybugs; see its description in the discussion of scale that follows.

The best-known predator for mealybugs is an Australian lady beetle, *Cryptolaemus montrouzieri*. It is relatively expensive and needs both high mealybug populations and a high release rate to be effective. However, the lady beetles feed on all stages of the insect, and they have been used successfully in home greenhouses and conservatories.

Scale

Description

Scale insects are appropriately named for their outer covering, which forms a protective shield for the insects. Some types of scale insects have a soft outer coating that looks like cotton; the type that appears on tropical fruit plants is usually an armored scale, which forms a hard, waxy brown shield. These shieldlike brown bumps appear on the undersides of leaves and along the stems. The bumps are a protective shell that shelters the soft-bodied scale insects within. Scales are usually introduced by bringing infested plants into a collection.

Telltale Signs

Along with the brown bumps, black sooty mold on leaves can be a sign of scale infestation. The life cycle of scale insects involves an egg, crawler, soft shell stage, and hard shell stage. The hard shell stage is the mature form. The insects lay their eggs in the protection of the scale shell, making them hard to control. Crawlers emerge from under the shells over time.

Treatment

Control requires persistence. On shiny-leaved plants such as citrus, a cedar-oil-type product such as Ced-O-Flora is a good choice; it has low toxicity and is effective. Avoid using Ced-O-Flora on hairy or soft-leaved plants, as it will damage leaves. The growth regulator bupro-fezin (mentioned above for mealybugs) will also control scale. It takes repeated applications and should not be applied to plants that are producing fruit.

Neem oil smothers crawlers and the soft shell stage. Apply it as described in Fighting Pests with Neem Oil on page 146, but note that the frequency of application is different for scale insects because they are vulnerable to neem at several stages in their life cycle. Apply neem every two weeks for two months. We successfully eradicated an infestation of scale on our 150-year-old kumquat tree by using neem oil.

Slugs and Snails

Description

Slugs are soft-bodied creatures that can look like small gray pasta shells on a leaf. Snails are similar but have shells that look like seashells. Slugs and snails are generally more of a nuisance than a serious problem with container fruits. They can chew up the leaves of certain plants, such as avocado, star fruit, and passionflower, which makes the plants look unsightly. They prefer young growth and usually are active at night when humidity is high.

Telltale Signs

The telltale sign of a slug or snail is the silvery trail of slime that it leaves behind. The damage appears as holes or chewed areas in the leaves. During the day, slugs and snails hide in dark, damp areas. This can be the drainage hole in a pot or under the pot itself.

Treatment

One method of control is to physically remove slugs and snails from the plants and destroy them. There are also iron phosphate baits that can be sprinkled on the soil on which the slugs and snails feed; these baits are environmentally friendly and nontoxic to people and pets.

Other options are to place a band of copper around the pot or trunk of a plant; this will stop snails and slugs from moving up to the foliage because they won't cross copper. If this method is used, make sure other plants aren't touching the copper-protected plant, or the slugs or snails will cross over from the other plants.

Diseases of Container Plants

Disease symptoms will show up occasionally among your container plants. However, with proper attention to plant care, you can keep foliar disease and root disease from becoming a serious problem. Many times the solution is simply a matter of changing the environmental conditions. The trick is to identify the disease and then change the conditions immediately to restore your plant to health and wellness.

Foliar Disease

One advantage of growing tropical fruits in the North is that they're generally not susceptible to foliar disease. The exception is tropical plants grown in greenhouses or conservatories, which are susceptible to the most prevalent of all foliar diseases: botrytis, or gray mold. Other types of bacteria and fungi can also cause leaf spots, but they are not common and generally are found only under extremely damp conditions.

Botrytis. Common botrytis symptoms are brown spots or patches of necrotic tissue that appear on the flowers and leaves. Up close, you can see that these spots consist of concentric light and dark rings. When humidity is high enough, a gray fuzzy mold will appear; these are the spores of the fungus. Cool temperatures (45–65°F [7–18°C]) and stagnant air along with high humidity increase the risk of infection by botrytis fungi. In a house or sunroom where humidity is low, this disease is rare. Thus the best way to manage and control botrytis is to modify the environment.

Root Disease

Much like a sturdy foundation for a house, a strong root system is required to support a plant. Keeping root systems healthy is imperative for good growth and production. Some species of container fruits such as citrus, noni, and passionflower are more vulnerable to root disease than others. Even within a species, some varieties can be more disease-susceptible than others.

Stunted growth, chlorotic leaves, or a collapsing of the entire plant are all signs of possible root disease. You can easily check a plant's root system to see whether it is sick or healthy. Gently tap the plant out of the container (be sure the potting mix is damp before you try this). Once you've unveiled the rootball, carefully examine the roots on the outside of the ball. Healthy roots are white or tan, succulent, and fleshy when pulled apart. Unhealthy roots are brown, and when pulled, they fall apart with few signs of living tissue.

Several factors can cause roots to collapse. In addition to disease, repeated periods of severe dryness or high salt levels can be a factor. *Pythium, Phytophthora,* and *Rhizoctonia* are common pathogens that can kill roots. They are commonly known as water molds or damping-off fungi. They thrive under high moisture conditions and tend to infect roots that are soft and succulent. Identifying the specific organism causing a root disease isn't necessary because the management of all of these diseases is the same: create a drier root environment. The following cultural tips will help prevent problems with root disease:

Avoid overwatering. Allow the soil mix in your containers to dry out some between waterings (see page 130), and then thoroughly saturate the potting mix each time you water. This allows oxygen to enter the soil between waterings, which makes the root environment unfavorable to pathogens. Keep in mind that using terra-cotta pots rather than plastic or glazed ceramic allows soil to dry out more quickly.

Go easy on the fertilizer. Avoid high levels of fertilizer. Plants that are overfed produce large, lush leaves. On a cellular level, roots also become large and lush. This lush growth is more vulnerable to fungal infection. Reduced feeding in winter will help to bring susceptible plants safely through the season when root diseases are most prevalent.

Provide high light levels. Plant vigor helps disease resistance. Adjust the environment for optimum growth. Provide as much direct sunlight as possible. Keep roots at 65°F (18°C) or warmer. Most plants tolerate lower temperatures for short periods of time, but when root temperatures remain below 60°F (15°C) on a consistent basis, especially in low light and high moisture conditions, root disease can proliferate.

Let roots fill the pot. For plants that are susceptible to root diseases, keep pot size on the small side so roots fill all available space. A root system swimming in a large mass of wet soil, especially when temperatures are cool, is more likely to suffer from root disease than a plant whose root system has filled the container. It is better for a plant to be a little potbound. Wait until spring to do any repotting.

Troubleshooting Guide

Some of the most common problems that gardeners experience when raising tropical fruit in containers have nothing to do with pests or diseases. And many times you can find a solution simply by doing a little research on cultural requirements of an unhappy plant. Key factors include what light level a plant needs, whether it likes to be kept dry or moist, and whether it has a natural dormant period. In this section, we offer guidance and solutions for some of the most common tropical edible plant problems that our customers report to us.

My plant isn't flowering or fruiting.

Possible causes: Insufficient light; plant is immature; wrong conditions to initiate bud formation; over- or underfeeding.

Remedies:

Insufficient light: Check the light level your plant is receiving. If it's a full-sun plant, move it to a spot where it will receive at least 6–8 hours of sunlight every day.

Plant is immature: Wait and watch. Many fruiting plants take a couple of years to mature from a young seedling or cutting to a plant ready to fruit. A chocolate tree must grow to 4–5 feet and develop a forked trunk before it will set fruit. Under optimum growing conditions, this will take a couple of years.

Wrong conditions to initiate bud formation: Check the blooming cycle in the plant description. Generally, if a plant is a fall, winter, or spring bloomer, rest assured that it is waiting for the right light level or temperature conditions. For example, olive trees need a chilling period during the winter to initiate flowers. If an olive tree is kept in constantly warm conditions, it will never bloom.

Over- or underfeeding: Change your fertilizing regime. If plants are given too much nitrogen fertilizer, they will produce mostly foliage and not flowers. If too little fertilizer is given, then plants may not have enough strength to produce buds.

My plant's fruit falls off and never develops and matures.

Possible causes: Inadequate light level; plant is not large enough; weak root system; extreme environmental conditions.

Remedies:

Inadequate light level: Move the plant into brighter light. (We often see young fruit dropping off citrus plants because the plants are not receiving enough light.)

Plant is not large enough: Wait and watch. When the plant becomes larger, it will develop the reserves needed to bring fruit to ripeness.

Weak root system: Tap the plant out of the pot and examine the roots. If root disease is present and roots are shriveled and brown or black, follow the recommendations for treating root disease on page 149.

Extreme environmental conditions: Monitor temperature and move plants to a warmer location. Star fruit and acerola plants are especially susceptible to fruit drop if temperatures are continually cold and wet as the fruit is developing.

My plant flowers yet fails to set fruit.

Possible causes: No compatible pollen source present; lack of proper environmental conditions; poor pollination.

Remedies:

No compatible pollen source present: Procure a compatible pollinator plant. Some fruiting plants, such as avocado and olive, are not genetically compatible with themselves. Fruit set can be a hit-or-miss occurrence if these are grown on their own. When a different variety is grown nearby as a pollinator, fruit set is generally heavy.

Lack of proper environmental conditions: Check the plant entries to learn what your plant needs. Some fruits such as star fruit, acerola, and peanut butter fruit need warmth and sunshine when the plants are in flower to set fruit well. If conditions are damp and cool, then fruit set is light or absent. For the northern gardener, this means that the best fruit set will take place in the summer, even for plants that flower on and off throughout the year.

Poor pollination: Try hand-pollinating. See page 134 for details.

My plant's leaves are turning yellow and falling off.

Possible causes: Normal shedding season; severe drought stress; underfertilization.

Remedies:

Normal shedding season: Wait for a change of season, and see if plants produce new leaves.

Severe drought stress: Monitor soil moisture more carefully and change watering frequency as needed.

Underfertilization: If the plant is growing actively, increase the frequency or strength of fertilizing.

My plant looks like a palm tree because all the lower leaves are turning yellow and dropping off.

Possible causes: Drought stress; underfeeding.

Remedies:

Drought stress: Check soil moisture and adjust watering frequency as needed.

Underfeeding: Increase frequency of fertilizing.

My plant's leaves are turning yellow and there is webbing on the plant.

Possible cause: Spider mite infestation.

Remedy: See page 144 for recommendations for controlling spider mites.

The younger leaves on my plant are yellow with pronounced green veins.

Possible cause: Iron chlorosis.

Remedy: Check the root system for root health. If the roots are healthy, apply an iron supplement such as chelated iron.

My plant's leaves lack luster and are rolling and falling off.

Possible cause: Root disease.

Remedy: Immediately monitor moisture and allow soil to dry out. Move the plant into a terra-cotta pot. This is a common problem with container-grown citrus. For more solutions, see Root Disease on page 149.

Green leaves are dropping off my plant.

Possible causes: Change of environment; extreme drought stress; cold temperature; root disease.

Remedies:

Change of environment: Don't panic. Leaf drop is a common occurrence when plants are moved into a new environment. For example, plants brought inside from outdoors experience a drastic difference in light level and humidity. Citrus, star fruit, and papaya are a few of the plants that often drop their leaves because of this. Once the plant adjusts, leaf drop should stop.

Extreme drought stress: Examine the leaves closely. If some are crispy and dry, then drought stress is probably the cause. The plant may survive and produce new leaves if you water it well. After that, monitor soil moisture and change watering frequency as needed.

Cold temperature: Move the plant to a warmer spot.

Root disease: Tap the plant out of its pot and check to see if the roots are brown. If all roots fall apart easily when you touch them, most likely the plant is dead.

See Root Disease on page 149 for more information.

My plant is wilting but the soil is moist.

Possible cause: Too much love, i.e., overwatering.

Remedy: Allow soil to dry out; reduce frequency of watering. When a plant receives excessive water, the root system may collapse due to disease. Water only when the soil feels dry to the touch.

My plant's new leaves are crinkled and bumpy.

Possible cause: Low humidity.

Remedy: Increase humidity or simply live with the crinkled leaves. This will not harm the plant in any way.

There are brown edges on the leaves of my plant (edge burn, tip burn).

Possible cause: Salt buildup.

Remedy: Salt buildup is usually due to too much fertilizer (fertilizer nutrients are salts and harmful in excess). Other contributors include low humidity, low light levels, and disease. Here's how to fix the problem:

1. Flush plants with rainwater or distilled water to leach excess salts from the soil. Add enough so water collects in the dish beneath the plant; empty and repeat the process several times, using copious amounts of water.

2. Check your water supply. If your tap water is chlorinated, let it sit overnight before using on plants. If your tap water is very hard or you use a water softener, switch to rainwater for sensitive plants.

3. For plants that are regularly fertilized, reduce feeding frequency or amount, or both. After flushing soils, either dilute fertilizer by half or feed half as often as before.

4. If humidity is low, increase humidity by placing a humidifier in the room or placing the plant on a pebble tray and adding water to the tray frequently.

5. Check light levels and improve them if needed.

6. Check for disease and treat as needed. (See page 148 for information on reducing foliar disease problems.)

There is a sticky substance on the leaves of my plant.

Possible causes: Insect infestation; nectar dripping from flowers.

Remedies:

Insect infestation: Examine your plant for signs of aphids, mealybugs, whitefly, or scale. All of these insects excrete a sticky substance when they feed. See page 143 for more information.

Nectar dripping from flowers: If your plants are in flower and you find no sign of insect pests, then the sticky substance is probably nectar. No action is needed.

There are brown patches on some of my plant's leaves.

Possible causes: Overfertilization; foliar disease; pesticide damage.

Remedies:

Overfertilization: If you are fertilizing the plant regularly, reduce or stop feeding.

Foliar disease: See page 148 for information on reducing foliar disease problems.

Pesticide damage: Stop using pesticides.

My plant's leaves curl downward.

Possible causes: Wrong light conditions; nutrient imbalance.

Remedies:

Wrong light conditions: If the plant is a sun-lover, move it to full sun. If it's a shade-loving plant, move it out of direct sunlight.

Nutrient imbalance: Make sure you are using a fertilizer with a balanced NPK formula that contains micronutrients.

My plant looks scraggly — the leaves are floppy and the stems are leggy.

Possible cause: Lack of light.

Remedy: Move into higher levels of light.

Glossary

anther. A padlike structure that produces pollen; part of a stamen (male reproductive organ of a flower).

axil. The angle between a stem and a side branch or leaf stalk.

axillary bud. A bud found at a leaf axil along a stem.

balanced fertilizer. A fertilizer that contains approximately equal amounts of nitrogen, potassium, and phosphate.

beneficial insect. An insect that performs a role perceived as helpful by gardeners, such as pollinating plants, preying on or parasitizing pests, or contributing to the breakdown of organic matter.

biological control. A general term referring to reducing or eliminating populations of plant pests and pathogens using methods and products based on naturally occurring predators and parasites such as lacewings and parasitic wasps.

bonsai. A technique of creating miniaturized trees, usually in containers, through careful plant selection and training methods. Bonsai originated in China and Japan many centuries ago.

bud blast. The withering and dropping off of immature flower buds, usually caused by a change of environmental conditions or by a pest infestation.

chlorosis. A condition in which foliage becomes yellowish or pale green due to lack of development of chlorophyll. Interveinal chlorosis is lightening of the leaf tissue while the leaf veins remain green.

clone. A plant that is genetically identical to its parent plant. Clones are produced through asexual propagation techniques such as tissue culture.

cultivar. A common term for a cultivated variety, particular form of a plant that is developed and maintained through deliberate propagation.

dioecious. Bearing male and female reproductive organs on separate individuals of the same species. A dioecious species has male plants and female plants; at least one of each is required for successful pollination. *See* monoecious.

dormancy. A period when a plant is not actively growing.

dry down. A process by which potting mix is allowed to dry out between waterings, to the point that plants wilt slightly.

edge burn. Browning of leaf edges, usually due to excess fertilization.

family. A broad grouping of plants as designated by botanists; a subcategory of a plant order. Plant families such as the Citrus family (which has the botanical designation of Rutaceae) contain many genera of plants. *See* genus.

fruit set. The stage in fruit development at which a flower begins to form a fruit.

genus. A group of plants with similar growth characteristics. A plant genus is comprised of one or more species. *See* species.

grafting. A method of plant propagation that involves joining a piece of one plant, such as a bud or shoot, with another plant so that they unite and will grow together as one plant.

heading cut. A type of pruning cut. A heading cut removes the end portion of a stem just above a bud. Heading cuts stimulate latent buds to sprout.

insect growth regulator. A substance that changes an insect's normal pattern of growth and development, often in a way that prevents the insect from reaching maturity. Insect growth regulators can be effective for insect pest control.

iron chlorosis. The yellowing of plant tissue due to lack of sufficient iron in plant cells. Iron is an essential component of the green pigment chlorophyll.

jardinière. A decorative container used for growing plants.

leach. To remove nutrients from soil by drenching it with water. As water passes through soil, it carries dissolved nutrients with it.

monoecious. Having both male and female flowers on the same plant. *See* dioecious.

node. The point along a stem where a leaf, branch, or flower is attached.

organic fertilizer. A fertilizer that contains nutrients derived from plant, animal, and natural mineral sources.

perfect flower. A flower that contains both male and female reproductive structures.

perlite. A processed form of volcanic rock that is very lightweight. Perlite is frequently used in potting mixes to improve drainage and aeration.

pistil. The female reproductive structure of a flower.

pollen. Dustlike structures that contain genetic material. Pollen is produced by the male reproductive structure of a plant.

pollination. The transfer of pollen from the male structure (anthers) of a flower to the female structure (pistil).

pollinator. An animal or insect that transfers pollen from flower to flower. Also, a plant that serves as a pollen source for another plant.

potbound. Referring to a condition in which the rootball of a plant densely fills the container in which it is growing. Roots of a potbound plant can become thickly matted.

rootstock. A plant that provides a root system onto which another plant is budded or grafted; also called an understock.

soilless potting mix. A mixture that generally contains peat moss and perlite or vermiculite, but does not contain natural soil.

species. A closely related group of plants. A species of plants can be further subdivided into subspecies, naturally occurring varieties, and cultivated varieties (cultivars). *See* cultivar.

standard. A plant that has been trained to grow with a bare, upright main stem with a dense, bushy top. Some standards are kept formally clipped so that the top forms a perfect sphere.

stunting. A condition of shortened, weak growth, often in response to disease or nutrient deficiency.

synthetic fertilizer. A fertilizer manufactured from petroleum products or created by treating natural substances such as rock powders with acids or other substances to change their chemical structure. Also called chemical fertilizer.

top-dress. To apply fertilizer or soil amendments by spreading the material evenly over the soil surface around a plant or plants.

variety. A variant of a plant species that has evolved naturally, rather than by deliberate plant breeding efforts.

vesicle. A bladderlike sac that can be filled with juice or other fluid or with air.

Resources

Butterfly World
954-977-4400
www.butterflyworld.com
Seeds for many types of passion fruits
(the best *Passiflora* collection in the
United States) and other plants

California Rare Fruit Growers, Inc.
www.crfg.org
Largest amateur fruit-growing organi-
zation in the world; useful links and
lists of nurseries and local chapters

Flora Exotica
514-747-7618
www.floraexotica.ca
This supplier of exotic seeds and
plants ships throughout North
America

Going Bananas Nursery
305-247-0397
www.going-bananas.com
Great selection of bananas

Logee's Tropical Plants
888-330-8038
www.logees.com
Hundreds of varieties of tropical
plants, both fruiting and ornamental

One Green World Nursery
877-353-4028
www.onegreenworld.com
Fruiting plants of all kinds, mostly
temperate but some tropical

Pine Island Nursery
305-233-5501
www.tropicalfruitnursery.com
Large selection of tropical fruiting
plants that do well in Florida, many
good for containers

Raintree Nursery
800-391-8892
www.raintreenursery.com
Fruiting plants of every kind, some
tropical

Insect Suppliers

Gardener's Supply Company
888-833-1412
www.gardeners.com

IPM Laboratories, Inc.
315-497-2063
www.ipmlabs.com

Koppert Biological Systems
800-928-8827
www.koppertonline.com

Rincon-Vitova Insectaries
800-248-2847
www.rinconvitova.com

Acknowledgments

I would like to thank first Laurelynn Martin, my business partner, friend, and ally, for doing the literary crafting and sharing the journey into the world of plants together. Thanks to Richard Wallace, who shared his knowledge and enthusiasm of tropical plants along with the culture of horticulture. Thanks to tropical fruit grower Billy Hopkins of Hopkins Nursery, who shared his knowledge and collection with me. Thanks go out to my cousin, Rick Logee, who manages the greenhouses and uses his horticultural knowledge to grow our extensive collection. Plus, the entire staff at Logee's I thank for their dedication and hard work, especially Margaret Kahn for her editorial prowess. Ron Boender of Butterfly World shared with us his extensive collection of passionflowers. Also, thanks to my children, Elijah and Angelise Martin, and my mother-in-law, Barbara Glass, who has supported me in my many quests.

— Byron E. Martin

Many thanks go to many people who made this book possible. First, my coauthor, business partner, and friend, Byron Martin; his plant expertise, enthusiasm, and love for plants is always at the forefront. Margaret Kahn, Logee's customer service representative, turned into an editorial superwoman at night. My thanks also to the management staff at Logee's, including Sham ElShakhs, business manager; Rick Logee, greenhouse manager; Marie-Clarie Songhurst, office manager; and Sheryl Felty, merchandiser. Plus, our entire staff at Logee's contributed recipes and kept the place running while we wrote. Also, my thanks wouldn't be complete without thanking my children, Elijah and Angelise Martin, who didn't get much of Mom's time this past year, and my partner, Barbara Sarno, for helping me navigate family life, a business, and a book. Plus, her expert advice as a pastry chef was much appreciated and invaluable for checking, rewriting, and testing the recipes. Thanks to my mother, Barbara Glass, who in spite of her loss was still able to give words of encouragement and inspiration. And, lastly my editors, Fern Marshall Bradley and Gwen Steege, from Storey Publishing, for holding the vision and enthusiasm for this project.

— Laurelynn G. Martin

Index

Page references in *italics* indicate photographs or illustrations.

Other Storey Titles You Will Enjoy

Bulbs in the Basement, Geraniums on the Windowsill, by Alice & Brian McGowan.

The first comprehensive resource on the overwintering of tender perennials.

208 pages. Paper. ISBN 978-1-60342-042-6.

The Complete Houseplant Survival Manual, by Barbara Pleasant.

A stylish, detailed guide, complete with full-color photography plus advice for propagating 160 flowering and foliage houseplants.

384 pages. Flexibind. ISBN 978-1-58017-569-2.

Don't Throw It, Grow It!, by Deborah Peterson & Millicent Selsam.

Lush, vibrant houseplants from pits, nuts, beans, seeds, and tubers.

160 pages. Paper. ISBN 978-1-60342-064-8.

Landscaping with Fruit, by Lee Reich.

A complete, accessible guide to luscious landscaping — from alpine strawberry to lingonberry, mulberry to wintergreen.

192 pages. Paper. ISBN 978-1-60342-091-4.

Hardcover with jacket. ISBN 978-1-60342-096-9.

Tabletop Gardens, by Rosemary McCreary.

Designs for 40 dazzling tabletop gardens to inspire the indoor green thumb year-round.

168 pages. Paper with flaps. ISBN 978-1-58017-837-2.

Window Boxes Indoors & Out, by James Cramer & Dean Johnson.

Full-color photographs, step-by-step instructions, and quick design ideas for year-round window boxes.

176 pages. Paper. ISBN 978-1-58017-518-0.

These and other books from Storey Publishing are available
wherever quality books are sold or by calling 1-800-441-5700.
Visit us at *www.storey.com*.

variegated vanilla

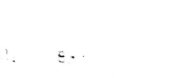

dwarf pomegranate